BASS GUIDE TIPS

Tactics Of Top Fishing Guides

by Larry Larsen

Book IX in the Bass Series Library

by Larsen's Outdoor Publishing

ISBN 0-936513-10-1

Library of Congress 90-063531

Published by:

LARSEN'S OUTDOOR PUBLISHING

2640 Elizabeth Place

Lakeland, FL 33813

PRINTED IN THE UNITED STATES OF AMERICA

4 5 6 7 8

2

ACKNOWLEDGMENTS

I want to thank the guides that I have fished with over the past 30 years, because I have learned from each one. Most were more than willing to share their knowledge and were excellent boat partners. With just a few exceptions, they have been honest, hardworking and excellent fishermen. They are indeed professionals in every sense of the word. I also wish to thank those clients of mine with whom I have shared information and camaraderie.

Thanks also to my friends in the media, those newspaper and magazine columnists and editors who are interested in sharing with their readers information about the BASS SERIES LIBRARY. I appreciate their kind comments. I appreciate the valuable contribution of my wife, Lilliam. Her review, layout and production assistance in developing "Bass Guide Tips" is much appreciated.

PREFACE

"Bass Guide Tips" focuses, as the subtitle says, on the productive tactics of the country's top fishing guides. Many of the guides mentioned in this book are "trophy specialists" while others are simply "bass guides" who catch lots of largemouth. Often the guides catch trophies one day and huge numbers the next. They are all excellent anglers and professional fishermen who are dedicated to providing the best service to their clientele.

This book, "Bass Guide Tips," should be a reference source for all anglers, regardless of where they live or their skill level. The "tips" within each chapter are effective methods that will help the reader catch more and larger bass. The proven techniques discussed are applicable to most waters around the country. Many, however, are not widely known in certain parts of the country. The reader should find numerous interesting concepts and ideas within the pages of this book to try the next time he is on the water.

CONTENTS

SECTION I
LURE & BAIT TACTICS

SECTION II
CONDITION TACTICS

ABOUT THE AUTHOR

For more than 18 years, Larry Larsen has studied and written about all aspects of bass fishing. His previously published books in the Bass Series Library detail highly productive fish catching methods and special techniques. He believes in explaining to readers the latest and very best tactics to find and catch bass anywhere.

Larry Larsen enjoys bass fishing as much as he enjoys writing about it. His angling adventures and research on the black bass have been extensive. He has caught and released numerous bass between five and 12 pounds and has literally traveled the globe to fish for largemouth and the uncommon species of bass. He has fished lakes from Canada to Honduras and from Cuba to Hawaii. He lives on Highland Hills Lake in Central Florida, where his bass boat sits at the dock.

The author is a frequent contributor on bass subjects to Outdoor Life, Sports Afield, and Field & Stream. More than 1,000 of Larsen's magazine articles have appeared in major outdoor magazines, including Bassin', North American Fisherman, Bass Fishing, Boat Magazine, Fishing Facts and Petersen's Fishing. His photography has appeared on the covers of many national publications. Larsen is a member of the Outdoor Writers Association of America (OWAA), the Southeastern Outdoor Press Association (SEOPA), and the Florida Outdoor Writers Association (FOWA).

Larsen has now authored 9 books in the award-winning BASS SERIES LIBRARY, plus a 260-page hard cover book for another publisher. Further information on the author's BASS SERIES LIBRARY is available at the back of this book. 🔲

INTRODUCTION

TOP GUIDE ADVICE

NOT ALL GUIDES are secretive. Sure, they may keep the location of their favorite hole from other local anglers, but most are happy to reveal their techniques. "Bass Guide Tips" focuses on the most productive methods of the top bass fishing guides in the country. Some of the guides are professional tournament fishermen, some guide on many waters and others are committed to just one lake. Sometimes, the techniques are regional, but they will usually work in waters all around the country.

"Bass Guide Tips" has been written as an informational guide for outlining specific approaches to catching more and bigger bass. Section I of the book considers Lure and Bait Tactics that many of these top bass guides employ. The section details productive methods for various habitats and conditions typically found in most lakes and rivers. Use of shiners and sunfish are discussed, as well as flippin', wormin', jerk baits, vibrating plugs and flies.

Section II covers Condition Tactics and explains how to catch largemouth from moving waters, hot and cold waters and deep waters. When the weather is tough, fishing can be also, but some guides are able to deal with frontal conditions, storms, high winds, etc. Chapters in this section discuss productive tactics for such. There is also a chapter on Brackish Water Tricks. Guides' observations of nature are presented in the final chapter.

Actually, the "final chapter" is not included within these covers. That is ... you actually going out and putting this information to good use. The last chapter is reserved for the reader's big catch!

SECTION I

LURE & BAIT TACTICS

- Shiner Man's Secrets

- Jig Flippin' Advice

- Tips From Wormin' Country

- "Dead Lure" Counsel

- Rattlin' Vibrations

- Jerk Bait Strategies

- Sunfish Kite Tricks

- Fly Fishing Prescriptions

CHAPTER 1

SHINER MAN'S SECRETS

Presentation Tricks and Bait Care

HUGE NATIVE SHINERS are an integral part of the productive methods of many trophy bass guides. Long-time friend Dan Thurmond, of Orange Springs, Florida, is one of the very best big bass guides in that state. He has used a variety of methods to employ the live bait and keep his clients happy. Over the past 12 years or so, they have caught over 400 bass exceeding 10 pounds, according to his detailed logs.

Thurmond and his clientele have also accounted for thousands of largemouth weighing from 6 to 10 pounds, and all were released. Fortunately for future trophy hunters, his clients are required to release the majority of the giants. To find a better opinion on maximizing the use of shiners for big bass, one couldn't go wrong by contacting Thurmond.

In addition to his full-time guide activities which puts him on the water 300 days a year, he operated a shiner concession for about 10 years. He was involved extensively in the operations of handling the shiners and treating them. Thurmond usually has his boat's baitwell stocked with native shiners up to 10 inches long for a day's fishing.

One of Thurmond's most productive shiner fishing methods takes place around floating vegetation. Today, there are many more floating plant species and communities in lakes across the south. Some are rooted to the shore and grow out over water; others have a tiny roots that hang just below each plant. The latter often drift with the wind until contained, but, even in relatively shallow water,

15

Dan Thurmond is a very successful trophy bass guide who use shiners extensively in his fishing. Many of his guide trips take place in the colder months when fishing live bait under the vegetated canopies is the best way to fool a big largemouth.

both are home to huge bass. Big bass guides like Thurmond are often anchored in front of a floating weed mass, submarining, or "running," shiners under the canopies.

Thurmond normally moves to the edge of a cove where a mass of water hyacinths are trapped by lily pads or timber in six to eight feet of stained water. He'll hook large 8-inch shiners through the lower part of the tail section, just behind the anal fin. That allows him to easily guide the bait back under the vegetated canopy. A few tugs on the line makes the shiner swim in the opposite direction.

"You have to swim your shiner back 20 feet from the edge of the cover to get a strike," Thurmond explains. "If a shiner won't venture back under the floating cover that far, switch to another."

Hangups occur, but that goes with the territory, big bass terri-

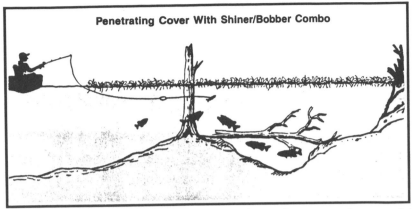

FIGURE 1 - When using live bait for working under a surface canopy, the successful guide will "run" large shiners 20 to 25 feet back under the floating cover. That's where the larger bass will normally hold, and presenting a bait in front of their nose usually results in a strike.

tory. Thurmond's shiners patrolling the darkened vegetation areas have been responsible for several largemouth between 13 and 15 1/2 pounds. Those are several reasons to try the method on any lake that finds itself covered with a weed canopy this year.

Bait Trolls

Another highly productive trophy hunter's tactic is trolling giant shiners with the electric motor. Thurmond is an expert at dragging king-sized shiners over any irregular bottom that has submerged brush or vegetation. Bottoms 8 to 20 feet deep are ideal for the method which involves a continually-running electric motor. Minor drops, though hard to detect with some electronics, can hold trophy bass.

Shiners tend to reflect their situation; when near to a lunker bass, they get nervous. Their jittery movements are a good indication of an impending strike, and therein lies a good part of the enjoyment of fooling big bass with the baitfish. Giant bass seem to sense that a fat shiner is restricted in movement and makes an easy meal.

"The baitfish will be perfectly calm as it moves through area after area, until it sees a predator nearby," a guide told me. "Then, it will

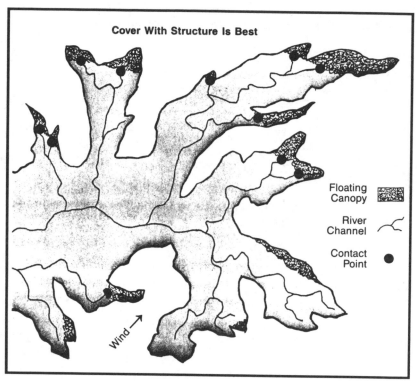

Cover With Structure Is Best

Floating Canopy

River Channel

Contact Point

Wind →

FIGURE 2 - Prime spots in a reservoir to seek out bass with shiners are those where an inundated river channel lies directly below a mass of floating cover. These are the most prominent "contact points" to find migrating bass. Note that not all weed clogged coves will have a definite channel penetrating the darkness beneath the canopy.

go wild trying to escape. That vulnerable state is what the big bass sense. If only our artificials could behave similarly - smoothly gliding along and then, at the right moment, frantically trying to vacate the area - they would catch a lot more big bass."

The shiners are hooked through both lips and placed about 50 yards behind the boat. Weight, weedless hooks, bobbers and the use of planar boards are options depending on the water characteristics. Many of the big bass guides in southern waters especially are pulling the big baits behind their craft. Trophy largemouth are fooled by these methods year around, but in the winter, the shiner is undoubtedly king of big bass producers in the deep South.

Dan Thurmond has developed a reputation for catching largemouth on live shiners all year long. For best survival chances, he hooks his baitfish through both lips, unless fishing under a floating form of cover.

Lively Bait

Since lively bait catches more bass than those almost dead, it's important to keep a close eye on the shiner and prevent it from struggling against weed structures if it becomes entangled. A shiner can wear out quickly if it's fighting against an entanglement. Thurmond will quickly replace a worn out shiner. The better working shiners will normally move and cover the area as though an angler was repetitively casting a lure. If the baitfish is not continually moving, then it's probably not going to come across bass quickly.

Naturally, good aeration and good chemicals, such as Shiner Life or Catch and Release, are a necessity when treating the shiner for optimal life and maximum usage. Thurmond uses Catch and Release formula for the bass brought aboard. The chemicals are very important in conserving the baitfish. Shiners in captivity, whether in a live well or commercial bait tank, are under stress. They are hyperactive, which not only increases their metabolism and use of oxygen, but also makes them more prone to injury as they swim into things or try to "jump" out of the confinement.

19

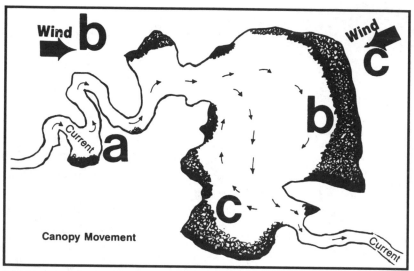

FIGURE 3 - Both wind and currents affect the movement of a weed canopy in a natural lake. Current alone will push the floating plants along until they are caught in an eddy or are moved out of the current (a). Wind (b) will push the masses of vegetation to the windward shore (b), into each and every pocket, cove or opening. The plants (c) are pushed by the wind direction (c).

Commercially available chemicals produced by Jungle Laboratories and other manufacturers have a safe combination of ingredients which will ensure maximum life for the bait. Most contain chemicals which kill bacteria and fungus, stimulate production of the slime coat, and neutralize chlorine and other poisons (heavy metals, etc.) in the water. Some of the better chemicals also have a tranquilizing agent. They are easy to use and cost just pennies a day. The shiners remain healthy and are full of life when they hit the lake.

For those without access to the chemicals, salt and ice can enhance the conservation of shiners. During warm water periods, the baitfish can be iced down to a comfortable 70 degrees. With the reduced oxygen consumption and lower metabolic levels, the baitfish will last longer. Add ice gradually to slowly bring down the temperature and preclude any chance of "temperature shock". Use rock salt to alleviate shock possibilities and aid the shiners to maintain proper blood pressure. Ice and salt can be used with the chemicals mentioned above to keep the baitfish frisky and ready to go find a bass.

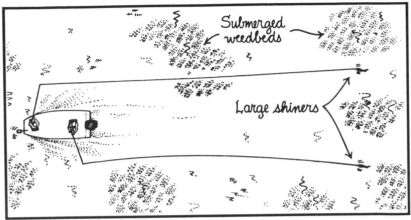

FIGURE 4 - A highly productive trophy bass hunter's tactic is trolling live shiners with the electric motor. Work the baitfish over irregular bottoms in water eight to 20 feet deep for best results.

Catching Your Own

While Thurmond doesn't catch his own bait, I've been with several guides that do. Some even start off the day by catching the bait first and then going fishing. There are two effective ways to catch your own bait. The most productive requires a good quality six or seven foot diameter (minimum) cast net. The other, using a cane pole with small hook and bobber, is the easiest way for a beginner.

Shiners can normally be found on the edge of moss or eel grass, close to moving water. They eat algae, so an area with plenty of it is important to find the large schools. An algae film can be found on eel grass in some of the better areas. In very clear waters, they can be particularly hard to lure near the range of a cast net. According to the expert shiner catchers, the native baitfish can also be more difficult to catch during a full moon than other solunar phases.

Early and late in the day are the most productive times to catch large shiners, but they can be easily caught over chummed and baited holes all day long. The size of the first shiners caught will generally reveal the typical size to be expected from the school, but all specimens from the highly oxygenated water will require continuous aeration once on board.

The initial step in the shiner catching process is to attract them

21

Many guides catch their own shiners at the beginning of the guide trip. A cane pole and bread ball the size of a BB is the preferred bait.

to an area by baiting it. This can be done by one of a variety of good baits; soybean cake, hog or rabbit pellets, dog food or anything with cereal in it. Even canned dog food with a couple of holes punched in the can to allow seepage will attract shiners to an area.

Bait The Hole

The cereal bait should be tossed into an area relatively free of weeds in about six feet of water for a cast net operation and ten to twelve feet deep for the cane pole fishing method. The best areas can be found by simply baiting about 12 areas and trying them all the next day to find the four to six that normally produce. The two or three best holes can then be re-baited for good expectations the following day.

Shiners can often be seen feeding on the surface in the pockets of heavy weed beds near the baited area, but the bait procurer can not normally go to them without scaring them away. It is, however, fairly easy to bring them up to the boat over the bait. This is done by chumming.

Although effective baiting requires 24 hours to attract a school of shiners to the area, chumming can produce in a few minutes. Quick oats, regular oat meal or bread crumbs,, mixed with water and dumped up-current from the baited hole should bring the shiners swimming.

The cane pole is the most common method of catching shiners and a bread ball the size of a BB is the preferred bait. The bread should be moist (fresh) in order to form a good ball, and the hook size can vary from number 12 to 16. The barb can be flattened for ease of extracting the hook to minimize possible injury to the shiner.

The bait should fall to about four feet below the small bobber. When the bobber disappears, the cane pole should be lifted and the shiner swung aboard the boat and quickly deposited in an aerated live well. When the shiners are feeding actively, a small white plastic worm, instead of bread ball, may be used satisfactorily.

Anglers with access to a cast net can round up several dozen shiners quicker than with cane poles. It may take one or two hours to net four dozen baitfish over a baited area. The net is most effective over holes totally void of vegetation, since aquatic growth will interfere with the net's closing. It can be cast over deeper spots, up to 10 feet in stained waters or on very cloudy days. Conversely, clear waters and high noon sunlight require a quicker net opening and shallower areas.

CHAPTER 2

JIG FLIPPIN' ADVICE

Jig & Worm Knowledge

THE SOFT-SPOKEN fishing guide steps up on the forward casting platform with arsenal in hand, an eight foot long, heavy action flippin' rod and spinning reel spooled with 30 pound test Trilene XL monofilament. He's ready to do battle and his equipment should be up to the task. Wayne Yohn of Lakeland, Florida, is after largemouth bass, big ones.

The expert flippin' angler has a pile of 8-inch black grape, blue glitter worms at his feet. Yohn is ready to arm his terminal tackle, consisting of a 5/0 worm hook and 5/8 ounce slip sinker, with the plastic imitation. A nearby "ammo" box lays open with a tray full of jigs partially covering several bottles of rind trailers. The jig-and-pig combination is for a change of pace, according to the productive guide.

Heavy cover such as bulrushes, Johnson grass, or cattails, is where the bigger bass are found, and Yohn and his clientele certainly catch more than their share. Equally important, this conservation-minded fisherman releases most of his fish. With dozens of largemouth over 10 pounds to his credit, that's important.

Yohn believes the most productive pattern during the first six months of the year is flippin' small bulrush clumps that are isolated within the emergent grass. The bigger Florida bass are usually holding in three to four feet at this time. Later on, during the summer heat, the best pattern will probably be fishing the dense buggy-whip patches or grass beds in four to five feet of water. He will

25

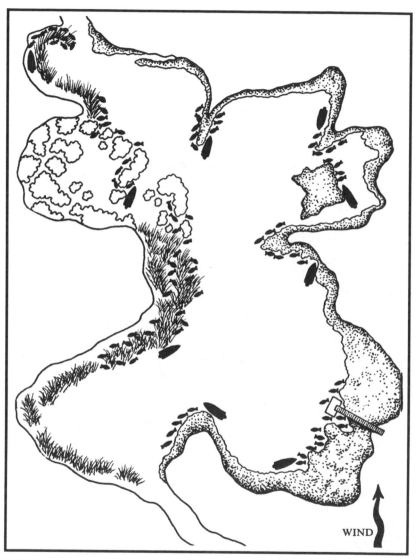

WIND

FIGURE 5 - Bass relating to the edges of dense cover can often be fooled by the flippin' bass man. Variations on the perimeter of a weedline attract fish and flippin' can be effective. The boat is maneuvered to within a few feet of bass-laden cover.

look for movement in the bulrushes or grass beds as an indicator of the presence of fish.

"A lot of fishermen will see movement in the vegetation and cast to it for a long time, without knowing that the fish there may be Nile perch," says Yohn. "You have to be careful, because where there's a large concentration of Nile perch, bass aren't usually present."

To figure out what is bumping the rushes or grass, look at the movement closely. Nile perch, or tilapia as they are officially known, travel en masse. They knock several stalks at once when they move. Seldom will an isolated fish be a member of the tilapia family. Large 'bumps' of the heavy cover are usually largemouth bass.

"Instead of a bass shaking one reed or a small clump, a Nile perch will take off and start a chain reaction," points out Yohn. "Bass won't do that. They are more curious and they'll sit there and watch to see what spooked that one fish."

Points and pockets in the cover draw the guide's attention. He'll move in close to that terrain and check the water depth and type of bottom present, looking for sandy soil. Bass prefer a clean bottom, particularly in the spring. Even if the area has decomposed pads or other vegetation, a sandy soil beneath will attract bass during the spawn.

"They'll move in if there is cover left and will fan the layer of trash off the top to make the beds," he says. "Fish know that the sand is there, and they don't mind going in there and fanning away the trash."

Bulrushes grow in sandy areas, and Yohn likes to flip a bait into them more than into cattails. The "buggy whips" are easier to fish because they are stiff and straight, while the cattails have leaves that branch off as it rises from the water's surface, according to Yohn. Most of the cattail patches also grow in shallower water. Both, however, provide super cover for bass.

The better patches of reeds and cattails to flip can be found by eye-balling the height. The good areas have tall vegetation growth due to the optimal soil conditions. The sandy bottom is more fertile, causing the reeds to grow to taller elevations. Bass prefer the additional protection from "high-rise" reeds, and Yohn prefers to place his baits where the most bass can be found.

The multi-lake guide considers Lake Tohopekaliga to be his "home" lake, and flippin' its waters has been very productive for him. He won a 331-contestant Red Man tournament on the lake a few years ago, and a one-day Boat Tournament in which Yohn and a partner out-fished 142 other competitors. Yohn himself pulled in two largemouth over 10 pounds and several others, including a 7 pounder. The native Lakelander teamed with his partner to amass a gargantuan 60 pound, 2 ounce stringer! The 14 fish caught, mostly between noon and 2 p.m., were taken by flippin' "buggy whips", as Yohn calls the bulrushes.

Precise Presentations

"The key to catching bass from the weeds is to effectively present the lure to the fish at the right time," says Yohn. "The presentation should be smooth and quiet."

Yohn begins the "yo-yo" type cast by raising the rod tip with the bait just off the water's surface and simultaneously stripping off more line with his left hand. With an underhand swing, he arches the lure in a pendulum motion toward the target. He controls the excess line with his left hand which moves back to the reel as the lure pulls out the stripped line.

His left hand slows the lure's descent and allows it to drop noiselessly beneath the surface. The reed clump is generally nearby and the amount of line out at the termination of the drop is usually less than 12 feet. Yohn feels that line control is extremely important for anglers beginning to flip.

When flippin' in heavy cover, Yohn will turn his line loose and try to let the lure hit the bottom directly below the surface entrance. Once the lure has softly plummeted to the bottom in heavy vegetation, Yohn 'checks it'. He lifts up on the rod lightly to determine if a fish has hit the bait while the line was slack. The angler should know whether or not a bass is in possession prior to his jigging the bait up and down.

At times, Yohn will let the bait sit still for ten seconds before he checks it. Then he'll lift it up slowly and let it fall back to the bottom again. He'll let the bait sit once again for several seconds. You might have to do that three or four times to entice a Florida bass during the spring, according to Yohn.

Huge bass bury themselves in dense vegetation, as Dave Fuerst found out. Flipping a weighted worm or jig-and-pig into a clump of vegetation can reward an angler with a great battle.

Yohn normally prefers to let the fish mouth the bait for two or three seconds before he sets the hook. If he feels a solid hit, however, he will set back on the rod immediately. Most strikes will be of the proverbial "tap" nature though, and he'll wait a few seconds before checking to see if the bass still has it.

"A lot of times, largemouth will lightly tap the lure to see what reaction he'll get out of the bait," says Yohn. "Then, he'll turn around and come back, and hit it again. Bass are real curious when that bait first gets down there. I've watched them in clear water and they'll gather around and look at the bait when you first put it down there, waiting for it to do something."

"When you move the bait, a couple of things usually happen," advises Yohn. "The sudden movement of the bait will scare one or two of the bass away, but it will make the rest of them more aggressive. They will swim up closer to get a better look at it," he says. "Then, when you move the bait one more time, one of the bass will hit it. I believe that such behavior on the bait's part makes that fish mad."

"You have to picture in your mind what happens down there," he says. "The bass is a little startled when the lure first falls to the bottom. An aggressive bass may hit it out of instinct as a reaction when it first drops, and at other times bass will hit it out of curiosity."

Subtle Movements

"On a summer pattern, just drop the lure in the reeds, and as it is sinking, you'll see the stalks shake. Or you may even feel a bass through the rod as it catches the bait on the fall," advises Yohn. "If not, watch your line and it will start moving off. All you have to do is set then!"

"If that bush shakes when the lures fall to the bottom, the chances are that the bass has it, " he says. "You can then go ahead and set the hook, because he's got it."

Yohn believes in watching the line at all times. The slightest twitch usually denotes a strike and Yohn sets the hook. During the first six months of the year, bass seldom hit the bait on the fall, according to the flippin' pro. They'll normally hit it as you move the bait. They are spooky then. If the bait drops too fast, it may scare the fish, so Yohn will lighten the sinker weight to make it fall slower. The

Bass love thick cover, and the man that drops a jig or worm beside the right habitat can reap dividends, as the author shows. The thicker below-water mass of vegetation, the more productive it is to anglers employing the flippin' technique.

jig-and-pig work well under these conditions of lower than normal water temperatures, particularly four feet below the surface.

Flippin' is a good technique to use with a pork rind, because if the "pig" dries out, you may as well toss it in the trash. You have to keep the bait wet and pliable for it to be effective. Flippin' maximizes the lure's time under the surface, and coincidentally, in the productive strike zone!

I traveled with Yohn to a small natural lake to view the master at work. We quickly established a pattern and found flippin' the buggy whips surrounded by thinner grass on the inside of huge beds of vegetation to be most productive. It was the same one that he used the previous weekend to finish first and third in tournament competition.

Our lures probed the isolated bulrushes as Yohn moved the boat through acres of Johnson grass. It seemed as though each grass stalk was the landing pad for 200 or 300 blind mosquitoes. We were inundated with thousands of them as the boat moved between each clump of bulrushes. With absolutely no breeze to prevent their "clustering" about us, our flippin' the area was a task. Breathing was too.

Fortunately, we each managed to pull in two largemouth during the period between noon and 3 p.m. Yohn, with a deserved big bass reputation, captured lunkers of 6 1/2 and ten pounds even. After several photos, both were returned to the waters to do battle with another angler some other time. I had what I needed on film.

Yohn's technique is certainly worthy of duplicating for the serious angler. He fishes both sides of a clump of reeds. He's often fished one side, picked up the bait and dropped it on the other side, where a bass was waiting. Flippin' is the easy way of checking out that kind of action.

Jigging Tricks

Another guide and expert jigging man is professional bass fisherman Woo Daves. The Chester, Virginia angler fishes a "twitching" jig in his home waters, Buggs Island, as well as while touring national tournament circuit sites around the country. Daves won his first major event in 1975 and has numerous top ten finishes since. He has qualified for seven B.A.S.S. Masters Classics. He spends over

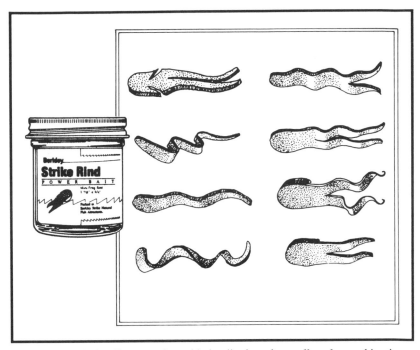

FIGURE 6 - Rind trailers are often added to jigs in order to allow the combination to sink slower. That's what fools bass, according to the guides. A variety of shapes and action is available at the local tackle store.

150 days a year on the water, usually with a rigged jig on the end of at least one rod.

Daves normally uses jigs in a variety of habitats - on lakes and rivers. He will often choose that particular bait over all others, especially when he is either looking for bigger fish or in cold front conditions.

"You have to concentrate on watching the jig and pig a lot more than with a plastic worm," reveals Daves. "You have to learn to set the hook a little faster too. Bass won't generally hold the jig as long."

"During a cold front, I once found some largemouth bass in a foot of crystal clear water near the dam," he says. They weren't supposed to be there. Local anglers were spreading the word that in order to catch largemouth bass after a front, you would have to run up the river."

Daves fished his jig and pig lure around any object that he came across. He even caught a largemouth bass from around an abandoned clothes basket that was sitting in shallow water. Another keeper-size fish was caught around an irrigation pump that a waterfront homeowner had installed in the lake. Apparently, anything that offered shade, such as a boat dock, would hold fish.

"I caught a quick limit of 12 to 14-inch long spotted bass with a small plastic worm early in the day and then went to a jig and pig for largemouth," says Daves. "The bigger bait would sink slower, and that fooled the largemouth."

The Virginia pro has caught spotted bass on jigs, but in doing so, he usually had to go to an 1/8 ounce lead head and trim the skirt. He normally cut the rubber legs back to a point almost even with the hook. Daves uses a smaller jig with 1/0 hook on it if he is trying to catch spots.

Jig Modifications

How Daves trims the skirt is interesting. He does so in a "Christmas tree" pattern. He will hold the jig vertical by the lead head with the rubber skirt hanging, and then he will trim on an angle. Daves makes a "V" shape of the skirt's bottom, trimming it on a short angle to the rear and a long angle to the front.

"When the jig hits the bottom, the short legs will pop out and you will get about three movements," he says. "I like to take my pork trailer and also split it. The more movement that the bait has, the more comfortable I feel about it attracting a bass."

"I prefer to cast my jigs, so I really don't want the model with the flippin' hook," explains Daves. "That hook is fine for flippin' and close-in work but not for long-distance casting. It's a lot harder to drive that big hook into a fish."

"Another major change that I make is to the weedguard," says the professional. "I will take the fiber guard and split it outward, so that there are, in effect, two guards. There might be 20 fibers sticking out on each side which I will then bend back up over the jig's head just as far as I can."

Daves will hold them in that position for a minute or so before releasing his grip. When the fibers move back toward their initial position, they will be aligned in a "fan-tail" effect, still guarding the hook. When the jig is pulled through dense bushes or vegetation, the fibers oriented to the side will prevent hangups much better than the original guard, according to the Virginia guide.

That particular modification will last quite a while, but not for the entire day. Daves advises that the fiber guard will probably have to be re-shaped three or four times over a long day's outing when fishing in heavy cover. Of course, the number of largemouth chewing on the bait will have an effect on the fiber's protective shape.

Another important procedure in Daves' successful jig fishing is to sharpen the hooks on all baits, prior to heading for the lake. He will even sharply hone jigs with factory-installed "lazer point" hooks. He considers that vital to successfully setting the hook.

CHAPTER 3

TIPS FROM WORMIN' COUNTRY

Pointers, Skippers and Pitchers

THREE FLORIDA GUIDES are especially knowledgeable about how to fish plastic worms. In a state where the majority of guides fish either the worm or live shiners, it is difficult to make a name for yourself. Everyone in the sunshine state seems to be a worm fisherman, but these guides are the cream of the crop.

The three-some, Doug Gilley, Dave Hoy and Manuel Spencer, have many years of Florida wormin' under their belt, and their performance on the water reflects this. All three men have tried their hand at tournament fishing and have done well, and all know how to put their fishing companions on fish.

Doug Gilley from Winter Springs, Florida, frequently fishes and guides on the Kissimmee River Chain and upper St. Johns River. Most avid bass chasers have heard of Gilley. He has been a mainstay at the top of tournament standings throughout the state. This angler fishes many local and regional tournaments each year in conjunction with his boat and tackle rep duties and guide ventures. Gilley has won numerous state and regional events, but he derived the most recognition from a $100,000 victory in a Super B.A.S.S. III Tournament held on the St. Johns.

"I was on an early summer worm pattern," says Gilley. "The bass were on the points that had eel grass with about two foot of water on them."

He actually had found three points during tournament practice days that were holding fish. On one of those points, Gilley caught

37

FIGURE 7 - A good early summer pattern is worming grass beds and brush in shallow water. A Texas-rigged worm with 1/4 ounce sinker is often employed by Florida Guides.

most of his bass. He was using a black with blue tail plastic worm rigged Carolina style with a sliding sinker, swivel, leader and worm hook. The timing was right; bass had just started moving onto the points. A week or two sooner than that Gilley claims he wouldn't have caught any fish on that pattern. In May and June, Gilley concentrates his efforts on worming largemouth bass. Fishing conditions then are optimal for excellent bass fishing.

"Another good early summer worming pattern is fishing inside the grass beds on large natural lakes," says Gilley. "Scattered grass away from the shoreline is ideal for this light line do-nothing technique. You just have to drift into the beds with the wind."

"I'll use a small worm on an 18 inch leader, a 1/4 ounce sinker and generally 8 to 10 pound test line," says the pro. "Even if the water is clear and shallow, that won't bother the fish at all. If you don't get several strikes in an hour's tossing, you're not really on the fish."

It's not unusual for Gilley and his partner to get into these areas and catch and release 50 fish a day. Most run pretty small. You might catch 50 bass and one might weigh eight or nine pounds, two or three will weigh five pounds, and the rest will be good, solid pound and a half fish, according to Gilley.

"Numbers and sizes will vary. Some days, all you catch are four and five pounders," Gilley says. "Other times, you can catch hundreds of fish in a few trips, and not have a single bass over two pounds!"

Wormin' Habitat

Gilley regularly focuses his summer wormin' on river and creeks, because he feels that bass can be easier to pattern on a river during hotter periods. Bass will be holding on the reed patches, eel grass patches, and points, and they will usually hit a worm.

"You can generally pull up to a point, and when you know that there's been a school of fish there for years, you can check it out in about five minutes with a do-nothing worm," he says. "You would have to spend a lot of time with a conventional Texas-worm rig at such places."

"There are always a few fish on any dock, and you can catch them with this worm," he says. "You can also catch them around reed beds and eel grass in certain areas. In other words, if you fish enough eel grass, you'll find an area that's holding fish where you can catch them on a worm. In the winter, they seem to just disappear, but not in the summer."

In flowing water, Gilley favors either a blue black shad worm with a blue belly, or a black worm with a blue tail. When the sun is out, the expert worm man will toss a black glitter worm with a blue tail.

"Whether the seasonal do-nothing worm pattern is any good or not depends on the weather," claims Gilley. "While I fish year around, I prefer to fish in hot weather because I'll generally catch bigger fish. It's not difficult to go to some lakes and catch a healthy stringer."

Skippin' Docks

Another expert worm fisherman is pipefitter and part-time guide Manuel Spencer of Palatka, Florida. Spencer is an accomplished weekend tournament angler who has made thousands of dollars winning local and state events by casting plastic worm fare to docks and pilings. He also won a Florida B.A.S.S. invitational held on the St. Johns River several years ago and has qualified for both the Bass Masters Classic and the Red Man All-American Bass Championship.

The St. Johns runs through Spencer's hometown and offers numerous wooden structures along its length, but his favorite technique will work on docks anywhere in the country. For you anglers who have mastered high-productivity presentations, worming docks and piers can be rewarding.

Spencer will first work the outside support pilings and decking. He is adept at presenting the worm far back under the cross members by skipping it across the surface and through the pilings. His boat is positioned about 15 feet away from the pier or dock structure, which allows him a side-arm cast off the port-side of his bass boat. The bait is skipped as far back into the shade as possible.

"You've got to get the worm under there," claims Spencer. "I'll try to place it back as far as there is relatively deep water. If there are at least 18 inches of water at the back side of the structure, that's where I want my worm to land."

The avid angler employs spinning gear for accomplishing that feat and opts for a 1/8 ounce bullet weight, 4/0 worm hook and a 7- or 7 1/2-inch worm. A very important tip to potential skippers is that the worm must be pegged. To prevent the sinker from sliding during a cast, a toothpick tip is wedged in the slip sinker's hole against the line. That allows the weight and bait to skip along the surface better and stay together. Pegging the lighter weights is especially vital to an effective skip-cast.

Manuel Spencer is well experienced in worming large rivers. His favorite technique is to skip a pegged-sinker worm rig under any dock or man-made cover he can find.

Swimming Tails

The dock specialist prefers a curly-tail worm for his skippin' offering. Once the wiggler has penetrated the cover and settled to the bottom, Spencer will engage the spinning reel's bail while letting the bait lay for several seconds if possible.

"If you are fishing a dock with current through it, you have to start retrieving the worm just after it falls to the bottom," he acknowledges. "It's best, though, to just let the worm sit still a little bit. Just cast the bait upstream of the piling as far as you can and then get it out before it is swept around that post. It is sometimes good to drag the worm around the piling," he continues, "but you also can get hung easily that way."

For extremely low docks, Spencer will get on his knees and cast under the structure. It is here that accuracy is vital to fooling one or more largemouth. He'll usually fish the end of the dock first and then move shallower along the walkway to the bank. In his area, most of the docks are fixed with either a large platform, boat house, or pier house on the ends. A 4-foot wide runway leads from the bank to the deeper end.

41

On deeper support pilings, Spencer may alter his tackle slightly to quickly reach the right spot on the bottom. He'll cast upstream of the target so that the current-swept bait falls to the base of it. In 15 feet of water, he employs a 1/4 ounce slip sinker (pegged), a small, straight-tail worm that will sink fairly fast and a 3/0 worm hook.

Once the bait is on the bottom, the experienced angler will keep it moving along with the current at the same rate of speed. To effectively do that, he simply keeps his line tight as the bait is drifting.

Lightweight Pitchin'

Bass guide Dave Hoy of Lakeland, Florida, offers a slightly different approach to catching bass on short lines. He operates the Professional Bass Guide Service with partner Ronnie Wagers and is normally fishing daily in the numerous phosphate pits and natural lakes scattered about Polk County. His worming tackle and rig doesn't take on the often macho appearance of that a flippin' angler would employ.

"In thin, isolated cover, I've found the most effective technique is to pitch plastic worms on extremely light tackle," says Hoy. "The real key is to use line that is usually considered too light for flippin' or pitchin' in cover."

Hoy's scaled-down rig consists of 10 pound test line, a six-inch worm, a No. 2/0 or 3/0 hook and a 1/8-ounce bullet weight, rather than the fairly standard 20 pound test and 1/2-ounce weight. Many anglers who flip and pitch to cover use baitcasting tackle, but that too may decrease the productivity, according to the guide.

"I've gone through areas that have received a lot of pressure from other fishermen using heavy conventional tackle and caught several bass with the light tackle and soft presentation," states Hoy. "In clearer water, thinner cover demands a more careful approach and presentation."

A flippin' angler finds it difficult to get close to such structure, and with the heavy line, difficult to entice a strike. Hoy backs over 15 feet or so and pitches his fare to the isolated cover. He employs a 7 foot spinning rod so that he can adjust his distance from the target more easily and get a more accurate drop on the bait. Accuracy is vital, according to the guide, because a "key spot" must be hit, and that may be a 6-inch diameter target.

Dave Hoy's guide parties often are successful pitchin' lightweight worm rigs in and around cover. A bass like this could make about anyone happy.

Hoy prefers to work his worm and slip sinker away from the boat and not up and down beside it - like the conventional flippin' motion. The spinning rod and reel is vital, because when the bait is pitched to the cover, it will fall directly to the bottom. A casting outfit tends to make the bait "pendulum back" away from the point of entry and target.

"With pads, it's extremely important not to swing the bait away from them," advises Hoy. "You have to get the worm right down in it. Then, if a bass doesn't pick it up on the fall, it's best to let the bait sit there for several seconds. It's very difficult to do, but I've had to leave the bait motionless for up to 30 seconds sometimes to entice a strike."

The angler has to maintain constant contact with the bait to recognize some of the softer strikes. The light line allows easier detection of a soft pick up, but a good sense of feel helps angler productivity with this method. Aiding that sense of feel is the fact that Hoy often does not use a pegged sinker.

43

Many anglers will take a toothpick and jam it into the sinker beside the line to secure the weight. About 50 percent of the time, Hoy will not peg his sinker. To him, that makes a big difference for fish that may be a little skittish.

"It's a pain in the rump to flip or pitch a non-pegged sinker rig, because you'll have more than your share of entanglements," acknowledges Hoy. "But seldom will there be bass on a piece of cover and not take a bait with the sliding sinker. I feel like the sinker reaching the bottom earlier than the worm causes the fish to respond better. They have more time to watch the worm settle slowly to the bottom them."

Cover Considerations

The guide uses the wind to push him toward the pitchin' target and minimizes operation of the trolling motor. Hoy would rather have the boat in the proper position and make one soft pitch than barrel on into a piece of cover and try to make five or six flips. It's that first pitch or flip that's always the most important one when you are fishing isolated cover.

Isolated reeds and cattails are prime cover during pre-spawn and spawning times for the bass expert. Lily pads are another of Hoy's favorite cover for using the light-line pitchin' technique. Water three to five feet deep seems ideal for this highly productive method.

The bass can be thick on the clumps of vegetation, but the convention flippin' angler just won't catch them. Hoy will often move in behind such fishermen and catch several from each clump. On a reed clump, he'll look for one or two stalks lying away from the main body which may consist of 10 or 12 reeds or more. He'll place his bait right on the two errant stalks to settle to the bottom.

Once you have explored the isolated cover, then work your way back into the thicker stuff, Hoy suggests. Don't worry about the light line, because you have to get the fish on before you get them out.

With the light tackle, Hoy employs a quick "pop-type" hook set. The smaller hook will allow better penetration, but the angler must respect the light line in emergent vegetation. He'll then maintain pressure on the largemouth until he can reach down and pick it up.

"The bass may bury itself or become entangled in the cover," he points out. "It will wear itself down when it has become tied up. Do

Guide Dave Hoy and Bill Cork, Public Relations Director for Plano Tackle Boxess found this ten pounder in isolated cover.

not try to horse the fish out of the heavy cover with such light tackle. On isolated cover, that bass may very well move directly out to open water, and the job of landing it is easy then."

"Using the conventional flippin' technique and just ripping a bass out of the cover won't work with the lighter tackle," adds Hoy. "Let the rod and cover work for you, and this technique will catch plenty of largemouth."

CHAPTER 4

"DEAD LURE" COUNSEL

Slow Death Presentations

SPEED CONTROL is the one area that most fishermen have trouble with, even professional guides. If an angler can figure out how the weather and other variables affect the bass and adjust their retrieval speed accordingly, they'll catch more fish.

There are keys to knowing when slow is better. Working a bait extremely slow is difficult for most anglers. You can't cover a lot of water, nor present the lure to as many bass. Weekend anglers seem intent on "getting on with the program." They want to cover as much water as possible in their minimal time available. Even professional tournament anglers avoid presentations such as "dead worming" due to inherent slowness. Guides who are on the water daily, however, have found the slow approach best for bass that may be "out of the mood."

There are advantages to being slow on the retrieve, and many anglers overlook them. Generally, the slower you fish a bait, the larger the average size of the bass. Bigger fish are considered to be more educated and/or lazier. It takes them a little longer to make up their mind, whether intentional or not. It stands to reason then, that if you can keep the lure in the strike zone a little longer, you are going to agitate some of the bigger bass to bite.

Also look at the historical catches of the various lures. Some of the most productive big bass baits are slow-moving baits, while some of the more effective fast lures primarily catch lots of smaller bass.

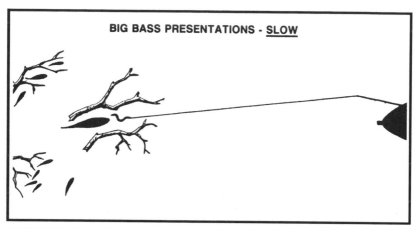

FIGURE 8 - Generally, the slower you fish a bait, the larger the average size of the bass. Bigger fish are usually less aggressive than smaller ones. It takes the lunkers a little longer to make up their mind, whether intentional or not. It stands to reason then, that if you can keep the lure in the strike zone a little longer, you are going to agitate some of the bigger bass to bite.

Obviously, there are exceptions, but the percentages seem to bear out such a conclusion.

Guide Jack Westberry knows that "slow is often better." He regularly utilizes "dead worming" over the hydrilla beds found extensively in shallow waters all over the southern U.S. The Tampa, Florida professional angler has traveled the country extensively, fishing the Operation Bass and B.A.S.S. tournament circuits, but he normally uses the technique while guiding.

"When you draw a tournament partner, it's tough trying to make him fish slow," he explains. "Only once have I convinced a partner to use the dead worm method. We were fishing 8 to 10 feet of weed-infested water when I made a cast and decided to go to a heavier line. I laid my rod down, got out another rig with 20 pound line, and about the time that I finished tying on the lure, my partner noticed something funny going on with the first rig."

Westberry and his partner were both fishing off the back platform, so he ran back to discover that there was a 3 pounder peeling line from his reel spool. The worm must have been sitting still for two or three minutes, according to the former university engineering professor.

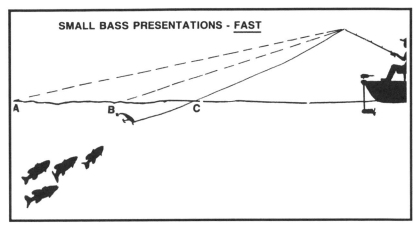

FIGURE 9 - Smaller fish have higher metabolisms and are much more competitive for food. They expend more energy in search of food, because they often have their brothers and sisters in hot pursuit of the same morsel. A faster lure (moving from point A to C) is usually highly effective on the smaller of the clan.

The same thing happened again as they were about to leave the spot. Westberry caught another 3 pounder when he laid his rod down to untie from a stump and get everything ready to go. He was putting on his life jacket when he had to again quickly pick up his rod and reel to keep a bass from making off with it.

To utilize the dead worm technique or any other slow presentation, the angler has to have a lot of patience. It's also helpful to have knowledge of what that bait is doing while sitting on the bottom.

The worm won't be laying perfectly still with a fish running up beside it. You can put a worm in any swimming pool and try to ease your foot up to that worm. You can't do it without moving the worm. The average angler may think a dead worm is not moving, but if a bass is there, the bait is moving ever so slightly.

If the bass tends to spook, swimming quickly away from it, or even if it just eases back into cover, the worm will move. Any minor turbulence in the water makes the worm wobble. When the fish moves away, back into cover, they are actually the ones causing the turbulence.

"If you watch the fish in clear water, he normally raises his tail up at least 15 times before he takes the worm," notes Westberry, "and then he just sucks it in. A lot of times, that's what you're feeling. So

49

Dead worming is a slow, methodical method to take bass from specific habitat. It is often used in the early spring and does require plenty of patience.

if you feel a tick, have a little bit of slack line between you and the lure, so that the fish doesn't feel you when he sucks it in."

Often the bass will just take it into its mouth and hold it. The angler may pick up the slack and when he feels the tightness, the fish pulls back. Generally, when dead worming, or "dead sticking" as some call it, the bass will just hold it.

Springtime Holes

When hydrilla begins to show up in the spring, it will grow sparsely at first with plenty of holes in the masses. You can look for

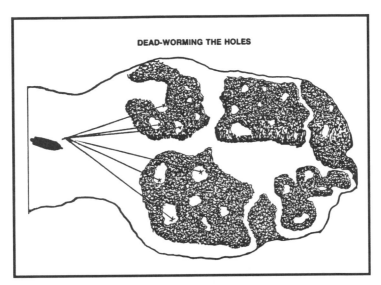

DEAD-WORMING THE HOLES

FIGURE 10 - When hydrilla begins to show up in the spring, it will grow sparsely at first with plenty of holes in the masses. Look for clumps of hydrilla with pockets in it and toss a dead worm to them. Pitch the lure to the hole and let it fall, watching the line as it descends. If you don't notice a tick, as the worm is going down, let it rest for up to 30 seconds. To move the worm, barely pick it up. If the taunt line feels "mushy", pause to determine if you can feel anything pulling back on it. If so, set the hook!

clumps of hydrilla with pockets in it and toss a worm to them. Westberry's favorite dead worm setup is a 6-inch soft worm with curl tail, 3/16 ounce sinker and 14 pound test Trilene line. The line is heavy enough to pull a bass from a hydrilla bed but not too heavy to prevent the worm from dropping into the pockets.

Westberry will pitch the lure to the hole and let it fall, watching the line as it descends. If he doesn't notice a tick as the worm is going down, he'll let it rest for up to 30 seconds. To move the worm, he'll barely pick it up. If the taut line feels "mushy", the 49-year old guide will pause to determine if he can feel anything pulling back on it.

If there is nothing pulling back, he'll raise the rod tip just enough to move it a little over the hydrilla. Then, he will let the bait sit for just about 10 second. Then, he'll pick it up again, and move it. If nothing strikes the lure, he cast to another hole.

"I look for holes," the guide says. "Most times when I fish hydrilla, I like to throw into something as big as a cartop. I'm looking for holes big enough that fish from different angles have a chance to see my bait. They should be able to see the worm as it sinks."

As the water temperature drops, bass often go to a winter pad pattern, and dead worming is still effective. Little clusters of bonnets can be fished the same way. He'll toss his worm to the pads and try to run it right down the stalks.

The way most anglers come upon the good dead worm pattern is when they get a backlash. Since that happens a lot in windy weather, that's when most fishermen go to the technique. Timing is right for the extremely slow fishing anytime the water temperature is 70 degrees or below, according to Westberry. In some states, that means six months out of the year, or more.

One thing to notice, when you do get a strike while dead worming, is which way the fish heads after picking up the bait. If he heads either back into the deep cover or quickly away from the area, he is running from competition. The observant angler can often cast back into the same hole and catch another bass. If the initial fish just stays still and chews on the worm, there may not be other bass in that neighborhood.

Line Thoughts

When you are fishing a short line, it's wise to have your line pretty much free of obstructions, where you can follow a quickly moving fish and purposely let it get away 10 or 12 feet before setting the hook. Doing so won't disturb that clump of pads which should attract another cast from you.

Westberry finds that he uses a lot of line while dead worming. He doesn't feel that anything heavier than 14 pound test is as effective. Using 8 pound line will draw all kinds of strikes, but getting the fish out of the cover may be difficult.

When dead worming brush piles, I'll also normally let a bass move off with the lure. If the fish runs out, I'll try to follow him. I'll take the chance and follow him as far as I can, so as not to tear up that brush pile. Then, I'll flip him into the boat and ease back to the brush for another cast. Under such circumstances, you can almost always catch another fish.

Another guide friend and professional angler that utilizes the ultra-slow retrieves around brush and other bass habitat is Denny

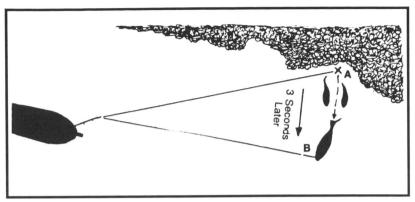

FIGURE 11 - When you do get a strike while dead worming, notice which way the fish heads after picking up the bait. If he heads either back into the deep cover or quickly away from the area (A to B), he is usually running from competition. The observant angler can often cast back into the same hole and catch another bass. If the initial fish just stays still and chews on the worm, there may not be other bass in that immediate area.

Brauer, of Camdenton, Missouri. His favorite waters, Lake of the Ozarks, often have bass that fall for the technique.

"Dead worming is a misconception in terminology, though" he says. "The technique can be applied to just about any bait you're fishing. It's just speed control, slowing down a bait and keeping it in the strike zone for a long period of time."

Predicting Fish Moods

The guide will continually try to adapt his retrieval speed to match the mood of the fish. Their mood is forced upon them by the weather situation, time of year, water temperature and other variables.

Productive anglers must adjust to the fish mood, and "dead sticking" is an effective technique to fish other baits like a jig. Brauer often uses the super still approach when flippin' and pitchin'; he'll put a bait in a piece of cover and leave it there for a long time, keeping it in front of the fish. If the fish are so laid back that you have to "dead stick" them to get a bite, they won't move a great distance, according to the guide.

53

The weather keys one into going to the dead worm technique more than anything. If significant weather systems move through and slow fish down, the productive angler will slow down his presentations, sometimes to the point that its called, "dead worming."

This technique plays a bigger part after a cold front, normally when the fish are knocked off their feet. The fish then can be neutral or negative fish and dead worming may be the only way that you can get them to bite.

In heavy grass, it takes a fish longer to locate the bait so the dead worm technique can be particularly deadly. You can let the bait lay there and give the bass a chance to "home in" on it. The technique can be used on matted vegetation, buck brush, willow trees, weed edges and other cover.

Dead and Peck Method

Brauer prefers to have some definition of cover to "dead stick" a lure. He may shake the jig or worm a couple of times and then let it sit another 10 seconds. He will continue doing that until a bass strikes. If the cover is such that you can get a bait up against it and just keep pecking at the cover, you can normally generate a lot of strikes. That sound, according to Brauer, drives the fish crazy.

If you know a bass is in the immediate area, you can agitate him into biting. If you have missed a strike at a specific piece of cover, seen the fish move the cover or have some other indication that a bass is there, work on him until you catch him. When fish are in a negative mood, you can force them to strike a lure, according to the Missouri bass guide.

Brauer will try to put the jig over a piece of cover and keep it right in the strike zone. He'll shake it up and down in one place, barely moving it, if possible. Then, he'll let it sit again for awhile. Brauer may let the bait sit without any movement whatsoever, for as long as 10 seconds. Then, he may twitch it again, trying to keep it in the same spot, without moving it out of the area.

"For example, five seconds is a long time to keep a bait in one spot," Brauer points out. "You try to keep the bait in one bush for five minutes and that will drive you crazy. You can imagine what that would be doing to that bass!"

Missouri guide, Denny Brauer, lets the weather conditions and other parameters reveal to him the mood of the bass. Inactive or neutral fish warrant the "dead stick" approach.

Swim and Dead Method

One trick that Brauer uses is to swim a plastic tube-type bait by a bush to the edge and then let it fall straight to the bottom. As soon as it reaches the bottom, he'll let it sit there without moving it. The bass have watched the lure come by the bush and free-fall to the bottom. They're curious, and soon they will move over and pick up the bait. There may be a five or ten second delay before they make their move, but it's usually a successful technique to employ. If you would immediately pick it up off the bottom, the bass may not bother to come over.

At times, you may have to let a bait lay for a long period of time. Bass will sometimes get very nervous and edgy. If the angler continues to move the worm through grass, the bass may become spooked, but if he simply puts it into the cover without bumping anything, a bass may come over and finally pick it up.

When bass are tight to cover and "spooky", weight of the lure can be critical. It's hard to keep a bait in one place with an extremely light bait. When you try to move it, the bait has a tendency to pick up off the bottom and move too far. To barely get that bait to quiver, you are better off with a 3/8 to 1/2 ounce.

Dead worming, or whatever you call the ultra-slow presentation is a fun method only because you sometimes get many more strikes than conventional retrieves might. Knowing the best times to go to the extremely effective method is vital. Otherwise, you may just get bored to death.

For anglers with plenty of patience and good technical fishing skills, the method is death on bass - slow death!

CHAPTER 5

RATTLIN' VIBRATIONS

Double Dose of Texas Techniques

"VIBRATING LURES ARE simple to use," claims Texas guide and professional bass angler Tommy Martin. "There aren't a lot of tricks to fishing them. Just bring the lure back with a medium to fast retrieve where it's ticking the tops of the grass. Keep the lure just above the hydrilla and the bass will come out and grab the bait."

"Normally, I make long casts over open-water flats to cover as much water as possible, he says. "Those areas with hydrilla growing up to within a few feet of the surface are best, and you don't need to twitch the rod or use stop-and-go retrieves to catch bass with the baits."

Martin has found that a fairly fast, steady retrieve works best, even in November's cool waters. Later, when water temperatures are in the 40's and 50's, he has noticed that bass will aggressively chase the lure even then. They will actually follow and strike the bait in cold waters when it is being reeled as fast as possible, according to the Toledo Bend Reservoir guide.

"You can't crank it fast enough to get the lure away from a bass," he says. "Very seldom will a slowly-retrieved vibrating plug catch bass. I'll point the rod toward the lure during the retrieve and reel."

The only other retrieve that Martin employs when tossing vibrating plugs is a pumping retrieve that works primarily in colder water. He'll generally make a long cast and let it sink into 8 or 10 feet of water. Then, he will pump the lure up with one motion and let it fall. He'll do that repeatedly all the way back to the boat.

57

Martin credits bass' interest in most vibrating plugs to the lure's internal rattles. The sound and vibration of the slab-type plugs are responsible for most strikes. This type of bait is especially effective in clear water, where it appeals to the three senses a bass uses to feed.

Noise from the hooks and other hardware can be significant, Vibrating baits develop over time a worn place on their belly, and that rubbing creates a lot of noise. Rattles also offer a cadence, though, that is often associated with the noise made by feeding or skittering shad. When an angler breaks up the cadence of his retrieve, or stops and starts the lure as it's coming back, he'll likely catch his fish with both hooks down in the fish's mouth. The erratic retrieve allows for a better hook-up-to-land ratio.

Vibrating plugs, both with and without rattles, have been catching fish for years. The longevity of vibrating, or sonic-type, plugs is based on angler success with the lures and the ease of fishing them. You can cover a tremendous amount of water with the slab baits, and anybody can tie one on and catch fish.

Most anyone can catch fish with a vibrating bait on a steady retrieve, but the lure is very versatile. You can cast it a long way. Most models sink with a designed-in action, so you can fish the lures a lot of different ways. You can jig the baits or rip them out of coontail moss 20 feet down and let them fall back to entice a strike.

Seasonal Colors

"When the water is cold, I'll use Rat-L-Traps to locate the bass," adds guide Bud Pruitt. "You can't go wrong throwing one of those type baits. They are great baits for covering water and checking out areas that don't really look that good. If there's a fish in those areas, they are more than likely to hit a Rat-L-Trap."

The young Houstonian tosses the bill-less baits around cover but not into the dense cover. He'll opt for the lures when working the flats or along long stretches of bank that don't have a lot of cover to pitch. He likes to cover water fast and selects a 3/4 ounce plug when after a healthy stringer of bass.

The guide and tournament angler often employs a slab-type plug when searching for bass. His experience at slaying Lake Sam Rayburn bass on an orange Rat-L-Trap is well-documented. In fact, the orange hue is one of his favorites for spring fishing also. He

The author has found that a vibrating bait is excellent in which to quickly cover water. The bill-less baits are among his favorites.

contends that bigger largemouth tend to go after that color. Pruitt has also found that the larger the lure, the larger the fish. That's particularly true of slab-type plugs.

"Select the fall-time colors such as a shad or chrome with black back in the 1/2 ounce size for the most action," advises Pruitt. "Toss them in the backs of creeks where the bass may be bunched up at this time of year. Once you have located the fish, then you may want to switch to a slower-type bait."

On a typical reservoir, the young guide will start at the upstream end of a creek and work toward the main lake. The fish will hit all day in such places, according to Pruitt. Just fish the Rat-L-Trap over the grass in 10 to 12 foot of water.

Other productive spots on impoundments for tossing a vibrating bait with a good chance of catching fish is around bridge pilings. Put the reel on freespool, and drop your lure beside the piling to the bottom. Then, rip it up. Let the bait fall, reeling in just a couple of feet of line, and rip it up once again. If nothing happens, move to the next piling.

Use the same technique in standing trees on a flooded reservoir. Drop the lure all the way to the bottom beside the biggest tree, so that the noise from the bait will bounce off the tree and attract a bass. You can "call up" a lot of curious fish by fishing both sides of the tree. Very seldom will you get hung up, but if you do the bait is heavy enough to be worked free.

Lure Size & Lure Colors

Tommy Martin employs various sizes of vibrating baits, depending on the type of structure being fished. The bass pro bases his lure size preference on the forage size at the particular time of year. In the fall, for example, bass will normally hit the larger size bait.

His selection of bait size is also dependent on the type cover that he's fishing. When it's extremely thick cover growing close to the surface, Martin selects a lighter lure so that it can remain fairly shallow on the retrieve. He'll use the 3/4 ounce bait for running deeper when the vegetation or cover will allow such.

Martin's color selection is similar to Pruitt's. It is most often based on the forage available. Martin prefers chrome combinations on his vibrating plugs, most often opting for chrome with either blue, green or black backs. All produce extremely well for him. In murky to turbid waters, Martin uses an orange fire-tiger or chartreuse paint schemes. Tennessee shad colored plugs are a favorite with this guide also.

Select the fall-time colors such as a shad or chrome with black back in the 1/2 ounce size for the most action. The size and color is usually based on forage considerations.

Landing The Fish

These type plugs are often prone to losing the fish that they hook. Proper fish playing technique and possibly model selection, however, can help to overcome the bait's ability to be thrown by the fish.

Once the hook has been set, Martin recommends keeping the rod tip low to prevent the bass from jumping. Don't try to overpower the fish on its way to the boat, because that's when it may get off. The less pressure you put on the bass, the less apt he is to jump, according to the professional. You should keep the rod low and the line tight.

"You don't want him to jump, because that is where most plugs are tossed free," he explains. "Invariably, the fish will get slack line, and the bait is heavy enough so that he can throw it. Use a two-handed rod and quickly hoist any small to medium size bass into the boat. Just don't ever give him a chance to jump close to the boat, because that's when the plug is most easily thrown."

A fairly recent development to help eliminate the tossed plugs is a sliding-type vibrating plug. Both the Hot Spot and Rat-L-Trap have line-through versions. The line is run through the body and tied directly to the treble hook which rides loosely against the plug's belly. With only the weight of the hook in its mouth, the bass is less apt to throw the free-sliding bait.

In shallow water, a bass will often want to come up and spit out the lure using the body's weight as leverage. With this rigging, the lure is free to travel up the line because only the hook is in the fish's mouth. Sliding versions of the bill-less plugs help some anglers who are losing fish on the vibrating lures, as does sharpening the hooks.

Long casts and steady retrieves are more prone to jumping bass strikes, thrown plugs and hang-ups. Over grass or in open water situations, Martin uses a two-handed, seven-foot medium action rod and throws the lure as far as possible. He'll use the pumping-type retrieve around very thick cover and over hard, sand bottoms. In standing timber, the professional guide and tournament contestant opts for shorter casts which normally prevent a hooked bass from getting hung up easily.

These type of baits are effectively during the cooler months in most waters. Stock up on the basic Color-C-Lector colors and put down some vibrations of your own. The bass will appreciate that.

Sonic-type plugs have been around for years, and they all catch fish. They are particularly productive when used around emergent grass.

CHAPTER 6

JERK BAIT STRATEGIES

Minnow Plugs are In Again

"IT'S A HIGHLY PRODUCTIVE early spring secret in our part of the country, and its use has been kept quiet for a long time," admitted Missouri guide Guido Hibdon. "Weighting the minnow plugs is deadly from February through the middle part of April. It is so critical to get the bait to suspend then. That is the way you catch those huge fish."

For years, the former BASS Master Classic Champ has relied on the slender minnow plugs, both modified and off the shelf, and he believes that they will out-fish any other type of bait during the spring in Midwest waters. Rogues with a common blue back are the optimal spring baits, according to Hibdon, as long as they are fished suspended.

To get a bait to suspend, Hibdon advises drilling them and then adding solder. Since each bait is different, you may have to spend some time adjusting each to suspend. When you can push it down in the water and have it almost stand still, the lure is properly weighted.

"Drill a hole in the bottom of the minnow plug just behind the front hook," explains Hibdon. "Then, take a tiny piece of cork, and push it into the hole. Put your solder into the cork, leaving a couple of inches sticking out from the plug and add a little bit of epoxy to seal it. Then, cut the solder off as you carefully adjust the buoyancy of the plug. When you get it the way you want it, you may have about an eighth of an inch of solder sticking out."

Line size is critical when using this rig, so you may have to adjust the bait further while on the water. For example, if you are using 14 pound test line and the bait is suspending perfectly, then you change to a reel with 12 pound test for some clearer water, the lure will probably sink. The stronger the line, the more its buoyancy will affect the plug's. The modification and employment of minnow plugs is very critical to success in the spring, according to the bass professional.

Regardless of how they are fished, no other lures have such a long, distinguished reputation for catching lots of bass and big ones. Slender minnow plugs have been around for ages. They have been productive from the beginning of their introduction, and today's new models travel to new depths.

The reasons for their success are easily defined, according to lure manufacturer Bill Norman. The minnow lures closely imitate the type food on which bass regularly feed. The baits have a lot of flash and look like food, so sound is not that important, according to Norman.

"During the spawning period, the minnow lures are great for a couple of reasons," he continues, "the food potential is there and aggressive strikes are generated. They may not be interested in feeding at all, but toss a minnow bait over a bed and watch out!"

Minnow baits with surface or near surface lips are productive throughout the year, if bass are frequenting shallow waters with heavy cover or in deep, clear waters, according to Norman. He's had bass come up from 25 feet deep to strike one of the plugs lying still on the surface. When the water is heavily stained or the bass are reluctant to feed on top, other options exist.

The deeper running lips have been added to the slender minnow baits over the past few years, as the angler's quest for deep, heretofore out-of-reach bass are being discovered. In Norman's line, his minnow plug runs between 15 and 20 feet when being trolled, depending on the size of line used, and on a cast, it will hit 12 to 15 feet.

"Obviously, what we are looking for by adding those deep bills are big bass," explains Norman. "Small bass will usually move a long ways after a bait, while big bass won't. By getting our minnow plugs deeper, we are trying to get them near those trophy-size fish."

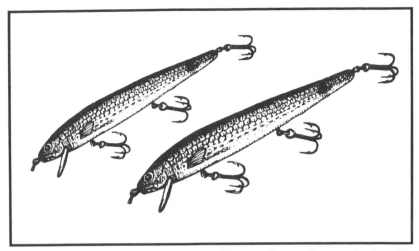

FIGURE 12 - Jerkbaits come in a variety of sizes, and most all are productive. Size selection is usually based on the capabilities of your other tackle (rod, reel and line).

"Overall, the near-surface plugs still seem to outperform those relatives that run deeper," he admits. "The shallow running baits just attract more bass. If you work them on top or just under, and work them very slow, bass will come from a long distance. If they can see it, they will usually get it, and of course, that's quite a thrill."

Herky-Jerky Baits

Clear water with at least three feet of visibility is needed for effectively working the minnow baits, agrees Lake Okeechobee guide and professional tournament angler Steve Daniel. One technique that he often employs in clear waters around the country is the "jerk" method. He calls the Bomber Long A his favorite jerk bait, but warns that it can be difficult to use correctly with this method.

"I crank the reel about three or four times and then jerk the bait on down," he explains. "I jerk hard twice and let it float back toward the surface sideways. Then, I jerk twice more and give it slack each time. When the lure kicks sideways or jumps backwards and floats up at each pause, then it is working just right."

"The minnow plug has to run perfectly straight," says Daniel. "The eye on a lot of them will be a little off center, and that makes

67

Brushy banks along a small creek allow lightweight lures to be worked in productive areas with a minimum of commotion. Such areas warrant quiet approaches.

the lure run a little weird. If it's running right, minnow plugs are the best bait ever made to trick fish."

Daniel prefers to keep the minnow plug moving around a lot, especially on clear days and calm water. The baits work best when the fish doesn't get too good a look at it. When you are jerking and kicking the bait around a lot, he contends that the bass knows it has to strike the bait before it gets away.

Whether the bass come up and hit it or not, using a minnow plug is a good way to find fish, according to Daniel. Even when they won't hit it, you will often see a bass follow. Just knowing those fish are there is a big plus. You'll know that you're in an area that's got fish, and you might change baits and catch one.

*A shallow-running minnow bait
fished in clear water on light line will
provide action that attracts bass from
twenty feet away.*

Timing Opportunities

The guide believes that the best time to fish a slender minnow is in the spring time, during March and April. You can catch fish all year long, but that's the prime time, according to Daniel. Fish are often bedding and will eagerly hit these baits then. They are cleaning out bedding areas and running a lot of forage out of these areas.

It was mid-March several years ago when the effectiveness of the small lures really impressed me. I was fishing Newnan's Lake in Central Florida on the coldest day of the year. The air temperature had fallen to the mid 30's as a strong 'norther' blew in. The 30 mph wind steadily shoved white-tipped waves at us, and gusts to 45 mph literally formed ice on our guides during our retrieves.

69

I happened to be participating in a small, 20-man club tournament or I wouldn't even have been on the water. Most of us had to spend an hour or two in a small, but warm, fish camp on the west shore. During the other five frigid hours, I was able to coax three keeper bass out of the white caps on the windward shore by tossing a spinnerbait.

I thought I had first place wrapped up with only one angler left to weigh in. After some playful hemming and hawing, he went to his live well and pulled out his single fish, a 10-pound, five ounce largemouth. The heavyweight was caught 15 minutes before the weigh in on a small, gold Rapala in a quiet cove on the lee shore. His ultralight tackle with 8-pound test whipped the trophy, which netted him first place and "Big Bass" in the tournament.

A shallow-running gold with black back Rapala is also Hibdon's choice in clear waters when he's not fishing one that suspends. The Missouri guide will normally fish it on 6 pound test line and twitch it around bedding fish. Hibdon believes that the little round lip provides the action that attracts bass from twenty feet away. From late April through June and again in late September and October, he'll opt for a jointed minnow plug.

"You could take a solid bait, and the fish will turn his head and move away from it," he points out. "With a little jointed one, however, you could catch him on it. In waters with visibility of six feet or less, I think bass feel the additional vibration of a jointed minnow bait."

Prime Areas

Brushy steep banks along a small creek or canal allow this lightweight lure to be worked in a productive area with a minimum of commotion. Such areas usually warrant super quiet approaches, and a soft splash down by the lure is usually preferable to a louder one. Small water bass seem to love these lures more so than fish in larger waters. One reason might be that a smaller food cycle generally exists in smaller bodies of water. Smaller lures are more productive than the larger ones, where the usual forage may be trim and fit.

Grassy flats are another springtime area that I feel these lures are specially productive in. During the spawn, bass may be in a very

70

protective mood but they seldom feed. Bedding largemouth do, however, slap at top water lures and such springtime antics can be the makings of a real headache or very productive. An angler that learns to wait until the bass has finally grabbed the lure can hook a bunch of fish. That may take four or five 'false' strikes, but usually the culprit will be hooked, if the fisherman doesn't move the plug.

Just let the floating-minnow lure lie still until the bass returns. There is normally a temptation, instinctive to most anglers, to rear back hard and set the hook when an explosion occurs next to the plug. Doing so, however, will usually result in the bait being pulled from the fish strike zone.

These techniques are not just reserved for those occasions when the bass are striking 'funny'. They should be productive often throughout the year.

CHAPTER 7

SUNFISH KITE TRICKS

Windy Persuasions for Weed-Bound Bass

FLYING A KITE with sunfish attached into the nastiest cover around will generate explosive strikes from giant largemouth, according to a south Florida guide. The unique live bait method allows you to effectively work the heaviest of cover away from the boat. Bill Walton's experience has proven the technique is highly productive in vegetated waters that don't easily yield their buried bass.

You can get the bait back into places that you can't normally reach, but you'll need steady wind and a kite specifically designed for the purpose. The most effective baits are bluegill and sunfish from the waters you're fishing. Catch the bait first and then go fly your kite for some exciting action.

Walton is a Lake Okeechobee guide who had been using kites in conjunction with live bait for saltwater fish off the east coast of Florida. He simply decided to extend that to freshwater fishing for largemouth. His big bass tally from the dense plant cover increased significantly, and so should other anglers' wanting to experiment with this technique on weedy waters near their home.

The specific equipment that you'll need to fly a bait to weed-bound bass is easy to obtain. Walton uses a Fishin' Kite, available through tackle stores at around $50. They come in four different models: light, medium, heavy and extra heavy. The latter has a looser weave. Other differences between the four are porosity of the material and cross member weight. Wind and size of bait being used is the driving factor behind which kite size to use.

With the use of Fishin' Kites, you can get the bait back into places that you can't normally reach, but you'll need steady wind. Bill Walton has noticed that his live baiting under kites has increased his big bass tally from dense plant cover.

A bridle is attached to the kite and a level wind reel is used to crank in and let out the line to the kite. The reel is mounted on a short heavy rod with rod guides large enough to allow a swivel to pass easily. Dacron line testing 50 pounds is ideal for controlling the kite in medium winds. A lighter 30 pound test is better in very light winds, though. A cross lok snap swivel placed 100 feet from the kite and another placed 40 feet back from the first completes the rig. That allows the shadow of the kite to be well past the bass when the bait is presented to it. Obviously, a sun overhead could pose problems.

Drifting Operations

The baitfish is hooked through the back near its dorsal fin without any weight attachment. The line from your reel is then placed through the snap and about 30 or 40 feet let out past the swivel. Let the line out as the kite goes up and out. The baitfish will remain on the water's surface as the kite climbs. Fish the bait just as you would a weedless spoon. Let it flutter through the heaviest vegetation for some explosive strikes.

The boat is allowed to drift toward the bait as it moves through the cover. If the wind slacks, and the kite falls into the water, you'll have to go get the kite and bait. Pulling it to the boat will probably only break the kite's cross members.

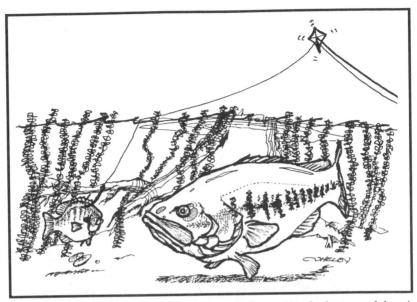

FIGURE 13 - The most effective bait to dangle from a kite for largemouth bass is bluegill or sunfish. Catch them right from the water you're fishing, and then go fly your kite for some exciting action. A trophy bass will often find the hand-size bluegill in dense vegetation. Giant bass are caught on live bait fished under kites almost everyday of the year. The word of the method's productivity is spreading among guides.

Once a bass hits the bait, knocking the line out of the clip, the angler should simply reel in the slack and set the hook. When drifting toward the bait, you'll be able to get the bass into the boat quickly. That's very important when fishing for trophy-size large-mouth in heavy cover.

The kite should stay aloft with a 6 mph wind or more and keep the baitfish on or near the surface as it "dances" through the weeds. Since the monofilament from the bait goes directly up to the clip on the kite line, there is seldom an entanglement with the weed cover. Hang-ups are usually just momentary as the baitfish is pulled onto some emergent vegetation.

The best types of aquatic plant growth in which to kite-fish are those that offer stalks near its base at the bottom of the lake bed and expand at the top near or above the surface. Even if the vegetation mats up during the summer, it will still hold largemouth below the

The specific equipment that you'll need to fly a bait to weed-bound bass is easy to obtain. Walton uses a Fishin' Kite, available through tackle stores at around $50.

surface canopies and on the fringes. Pepper grass is one such type of plant, but there are many others throughout the country.

Flying High

Walton and his clients have caught numerous big bass from the weed-laden waters of the south with the Lewis-designed kites. He fishes places that conventional techniques and tackle won't work. Such "virgin" territories are loaded with trophy bass that seldom, if ever, see a lure or live bait. He admits that the method is wild and crazy, but it works great.

More and more freshwater anglers are using kites to "fly baits" over grassy bass. The technique of presenting live bait via the kite was refined over the past 25 years by Miamian, Bob Lewis on saltwater species such as sailfish. People thought he was crazy years ago too, until his catches proved the method to be productive. Now it has spread from the coast inland.

The method is productive on bass just as long as there are weeds. Flying a kite over the heads of weed-bound bass has no season.

Largemouth are in the most dense weeds all year long, as long as the plant growth is in waters of adequate depth. Depths of six to eight feet appear sufficient in waters having two foot or less visibility.

Forage fish of all types frequent those weedbeds, so a properly presented baitfish struggling at the surface will certainly attract a bass from below. Shiners can be used under the kites but hand-size bluegill and sunfish are a little more hardy for dragging through the weeds. The bluegill will survive the livewell all day and be lively when called upon to "call up" a largemouth.

Drifting a live bluegill across a grassy flat is not for lazy anglers. You will have to control the kite and pay close attention to the baitfish action. Then, sooner or later, you'll have to yank a giant bass from the nastiest looking cover around. Call it crazy if you wish...or call it productive!

CHAPTER 8

FLY FISHING PRESCRIPTIONS

Schooling Consultation and Long Rods

"SCHOOL BASS ARE unpredictable and challenging," says guide Ken Daubert. "They will often charge right past your offering and bang their heads against your boat chasing after shad."

The flytier, guide and taxidermist from Silver Springs, Florida, has had a lot of experience with schoolers "on the fly." He has concluded the best way to locate schooling largemouth is to search for them until you find some. Daubert will keep moving through the open areas of nearby lakes when school bass are most likely to be breaking water; they're easier to see then.

Mornings, evenings, just before afternoon thunderstorms and sometimes during overcast weather with a light sprinkle of rain are his favorite times. The fly fisherman can find schoolers by searching for them all day long.

"If you don't see them in the earliest morning hours, they may move into that area later in the day," he says. "If you've encountered them in a particular area recently and if there are shad present, check back later that afternoon."

Bass that are actually feeding in schools and for the most part visible at the surface when actively attacking a school of baitfish, are a ball on a flyrod, according to Daubert. In the prime times, 30 to 40 largemouth can be fooled by the flyrodder.

"If school bass can be said to be predictable at all, the warmer months may provide the most action," says the custom bassbug tier. "I'll usually look for them in the spring and summer, and I usually find them. Ten pound bass are sometimes caught around of such schooling activity, but the mainstay of the excitement comes from the sheer numbers of fish caught."

The aggressiveness of the schoolers is what keeps Daubert going after more. He lives and operates his guide service out of a comfortable home on the shores of Half Moon Lake in the Ocala National Forest. It is there where he encounters many of his schoolers. The bass normally get active by around 8:30 a.m., and may school heavily until 11:30 a.m. At other times, they may be feeding at the crack of dawn or even in heavy early morning fog.

"In a heavy fog, your ears often locate bigger schools of fish behind you than in front of you," says Daubert. "With your eyes, you only see what's in front of you, but your ears will work 360 degrees. I've even had to go totally by sound."

"One foggy morning, I boated out to the main body of water, and I couldn't see much further than my bow-mounted trolling motor," he continues. "Finding any schoolers seemed hopeless. I shut the outboard down, and all was quiet, except for the sound of feeding bass. I couldn't perceive the direction of the sounds, and to complicate matters, there seemed to be several schools of largemouth in the area. The sounds carried well, but distances were difficult to guess. I simply ran the trolling motor until I got close enough to know where to cast."

"That was a strange but enjoyable fly fishing experience," says Daubert. "I caught over 30 bass before breakfast. It just goes to show that although foggy, overcast or rough weather can make it very difficult to find them, your hearing can sometimes make up for a lack of sight."

"Schooling bass may be on the surface feeding for hours, or for just a couple of seconds," he says. "If you are lucky, you may be able to consistently score heavily for days, weeks, or even months in the same area. They are definitely worth the search!"

Daubert has developed quite a reputation for catching and releasing bunches of school bass on fly fishing tackle. He relies greatly on his eyes and ears to locate breaking fish, and he often spots schooling activity in the early morning sunlight. The fly fishing guide watches for terns or gulls hovering or diving that may indicate a feeding frenzy. Even one or two birds are significant and worth investigating, according to Daubert.

80

Mornings, evenings, just before afternoon thunderstorms and sometimes during overcast weather with a light sprinkle of rain are Ken Daubert's favorite times. The properly-equipped fly fisherman can often find schooling largemouth by searching for them.

"I'll watch the surface for fleeing shad and for rafts of lazy, unmolested baitfish," says Daubert. "Later, the shad may not be so serene. I'll also look for 'nervous water,' which is something visibly different in the wave pattern. This tells me that schools of shad or bass may be swimming just beneath the surface."

Rod Weights

Daubert claims almost any lightweight flyrod will work, except on large school bass around heavy cover. Rods from 5- to 7-weights are most practical and a lot of fun on average-size school large-mouth.

"Graphite is the most efficient rod material," says the expert. "Longer rods of 8 1/2 to 9 feet will help you reach out for those schools that go down quickly. When the surface action fades, long rods help you get the distance needed for late and single risers. You have to use a long rod and long leaders to finesse some extended activity on stragglers in clear water."

"When the bass are gobbling shad near the boat, short rods are ideal," says Daubert. "The shorter rods of 7 1/2 to 8 feet are better for the fast action and as fish-fighting tools. They allow you to quickly catch a bass and get your fly back into the action."

Fly Options

Daubert prefers a Whitlock-style prismatic shad pattern for schoolers in clear to semi-clear water. He includes prismatic tape (sometimes called Flashabou) and marabou on his pattern. A tiny set of rattle eyes improves the bug, and the vibrations are magnified by the prismatic tape, according to the fly tier.

"The Whitlock pattern is effective on even the most finicky bass" he says. "You can stand on the casting deck with a pair of Polaroid sunglasses and fish it 'dead' amidst the crippled shad after they surface. Don't even retrieve it. Just let it suspend. You may never see or feel the bass, and you'll never catch him either if you don't set the hook quickly."

"The prismatic shad is also a great pattern for twitching across the surface as a cripple for finicky eaters," adds Daubert. "It's very deadly in most waters, the only exception being perhaps in dingy-colored water."

The central Florida guide has found that bugs which make surface commotion are most effective in off-colored waters. Poppers and sliders also work well at times. Underwater presentations should give off vibrations or pulsing sensations that bass can sense in the low-visibility environment. A simple marabou streamer fly with a green back, white belly and a streak of silver tinsel or mylar will be effective on clear water bass when they are schooling on silverside baitfish.

Ken Daubert, the fly tier, guide and taxidermist from Silver Springs, Florida has had a lot of experience with schoolers "on the fly." Match the size of the fly to the size of the shad being eaten, he suggests. Often, you can scoop up a few cripples for comparison.

The taxidermist/flytier makes a slim, fish-bodied bug out of flexible foam. He'll add a small latex curly tail for action, and finish it off with a realistic translucent finish that he's found to be very important in fooling sharp-eyed bass. The bugs adorned with rattling eyes work well on sinking and sink tip lines, according to the bearded guide.

"They are excellent for working right on the surface because the curly tail imitates the slapping noises made by swimming shad," says Daubert. "The floaters are also an excellent choice to fish on full sinking lines for suspended largemouth. The bass move into the deep-water grass beds between surface forays. Another thing to remember is to match the size of the fly to the size of the shad being eaten. Often, you can scoop up a few cripples for comparison."

The Line On Leaders

Keep several rods rigged with various types of tapered flylines when chasing schoolers. If the fish are seemingly unapproachable and you aren't getting a chance at a second cast, a rod with a shooting taper is your best weapon. The shooting taper line will allow a fast, long distance presentation for those schoolers that do not stay on the surface long enough to let you get into range.

The drawbacks of the shooting taper are reduced accuracy and the necessity to retrieve most of the running line before you can make another presentation, according to Daubert. If the fish are already gone, it doesn't matter, but if they are staying up a while, you won't want to waste time retrieving most of the line. A standard weight-forward taper is the best choice.

The weight-forward taper is slow getting started, requiring more false casting, but it has obvious advantages. It is very accurate, casts long distances and lays down neat presentations. It barely needs retrieving before a single back cast and second presentation can be made.

"The fly is out of the strike zone only for a couple of seconds," says Daubert. "Multiple presentations can be made for almost the entire duration of the rise. Moreover, with the deadly accuracy, you can tickle every corner of the zone keeping the fly in the area of the most heated competition. That's where even the most selective bass are vulnerable."

Weight-forward tapers allow light, long distance deliveries to selective stragglers even after the activity has subsided. If you can't catch bass in this situation, you're using the wrong fly, according to Daubert.

"One drawback to using this taper is that it does not cast wind-resistant bugs very well," he adds. "Bassbug tapers cast the wind resistant and larger bugs very well, and they get into action quickly. They don't get the distance of the weight forwards or shooting tapers, but they will cast wind resistant bugs quickly and effortlessly to moderate distances, certainly far enough for most situations."

Other Helpful Aids

A powerful, bow-mounted trolling motor on a relatively light-weight boat is ideal for fishing schooling bass. Since you'll be using your batteries to move to the schoolies very quickly, they should be fully charged.

"It's fine to use your outboard engine to locate the general area of the schoolers, but then turn it off," advises Daubert. "Racing to distant schools may bag you a couple of fish, but it also may prevent a full blown feeding frenzy from ever occurring."

Daubert uses a 34-pound thrust trolling motor and a 14-foot "double-wide" johnboat, which allows him to quickly get at breaking fish. The wide johnboat provides a stable casting platform, and his 10-horsepower outboard will even get the boat on a plane.

"The smaller outboard is actually a compromise," he points out, "because I often takes trips into remote Ocala National Forest lakes with my four-wheel-drive tow vehicle. In there, I need a boat that I can muscle around."

SECTION II

CONDITION TACTICS

- Moving Water Techniques

- Deep Water Lessons

- Hot Water Pointers

- Cold Water Pointers

- Tough Time Reports

- Stormy Guidance

- Tide and Moon Indications

- Observations Around You

CHAPTER 9

MOVING WATER TECHNIQUES

Unique River Pilot Presentations

BIG RIVER BASS are a different ball game, according to professional guide Bob Stonewater. With over 600 ten pound or better largemouth to his credit in the past ten years, it's time to listen to some of his thoughts, as unorthodox as some may be. His experience lays the groundwork for new, very productive techniques involving the use of the ultimate lunker bass bait, the golden shiner.

While he enjoys casting artificials, large shiners are the guide's choice for consistently catching monster bass, because they're a natural forage. Largemouth eat them year around. Stonewater fishes them over the same period.

"You'll trick a lot of 6, 7, or 8 pound fish on artificials, but the bigger ones usually want the baitfish," says Stonewater. "In fact, of the 200 fish over ten pounds that I've taken personally, only 19 were caught on lures."

"There are several things you can do with the live bait too," he says. Other than bobber and freeline fishing, Stonewater frequently employs a slip sinker "worm" rig, a submarine bobber rig, and the do-nothing Carolina rig. Each unique method for tossing shiners has proved highly successful for the innovative guide.

His "Texas-rigged" baitfish is worked off the deeper dropoffs and is very effective around structure, such as logs and brush piles. On more than one occasion, he's worked his crank baits and plastic worm rigs in such territory to no avail. Then he'll put on a shiner in place of the artificial and catch some tight-lipped largemouth.

89

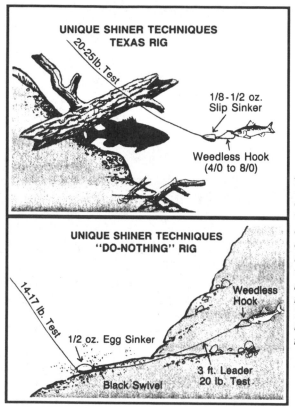

FIGURE 14 - Use the Texas-rigged shiner around submerged wood, over snaggy dropoffs or in other dense habitat. Fish it like you would a plastic worm. Use the "do-nothing" rig when slow-trolling along dropoffs. The sinker will stir up the bottom while the bait rides up higher.

The guide recently had a couple with him fishing such structure when Stonewater hooked a baitfish on his Texas rig and tossed it into the deep water. He commented that the shiner was the kind of "worm" he likes to use as the couple stared in amazement.

Stonewater had crawled the bait over a log and let it fall back when the rod tip was jerked to the water. He handed the rod quickly to the client, who tightened up and set the hook into an eight and a half pound bass.

Do-Nothing Bait

A "do-nothing" rig is also used by the shiner-fishing guide. The hook is heavier than what's normally found on such a rig with plas-

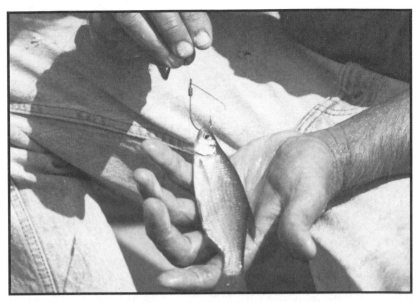

There are various ways to hook and rig a shiner for fishing moving waters. Most methods utilize a lip-hooked baitfish, because the fish seems to live longer in currents.

tic worm attached. The rig is composed of a 1/2 ounce sinker in front of a strong Berkley swivel, and a 20 pound test leader of three to four feet at the terminal end. It is worked over the same dropoffs with cover, and if there is a bigger bass there, the shiner-equipped rig will catch it, claims Stonewater.

You can also troll the "do-nothing" rig along the edges of dropoffs which are, according to the guide, easy to figure out in a river. The shiner moves along about three feet off the bottom while the sinker digs into it, stirring the sand. The line used can be lighter when trolling in open water. Stonewater uses 14 to 17 pound test for such activity.

Stonewater has another unique shiner rig for specific uses. On a broad patch of cover over deep water he'll use a bobber with a slip sinker in front of the shiner. It's a unique rig. The distance between the weedless hook and bobber may be ten feet or so. That allows the baitfish to swim up under the cover, yet keep it below the heavy vegetation. The sinker will pull the shiner back out without attracting a lot of tangles.

91

Stonewater is responsible for putting the author's wife, Lilliam, on her largest bass ever - an 8 1/2 pounder. His unconventional methods are often successful on river largemouth.

When the bass are buried back under heavier cover and are not feeding on the outer edge, which may be extremely deep, this rig allows him to present a natural looking lip-hooked bait to those fish.

Three Quick Strikes

Stonewater has found that once he finds a productive spot, he'll get three or four strikes and then it'll slow down. So, he feels that it's best to just move to another productive hole that he knows holds bass, rather than wait out slower strikes after the initial flurry.

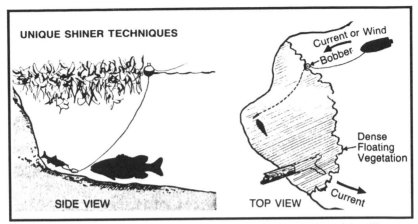

FIGURE 15 - The bait is worked into and under dense weeds. The weight will prevent the shiner from burying itself in the cover. Current or wave action is used to push the rig up against the cover.

"You can always come back and get the other fish," he says. "But your time is more productive if you don't hit one spot too heavily. You'll have more strikes per hour, and that gives your client a better chance of catching fish."

The guide is concerned only with trophy largemouth. That's what his clients are generally looking for and that's what his life is built around. He is just not content with bass of lesser proportions. His methods and learning have evolved from the goal of successful lunker bass angling.

A believer in big baits, the guide uses the largest shiners he can find, some even as large as 14 to 16 inches in length. Bigger forage will catch bigger bass, he reasons. On one recent week's tally only two of 25 bass caught weighed less than six pounds. Monster bait was responsible for such a record.

Offering a big fish just one big shiner may not suffice either. A 13 1/4 pounder hit two shiners on one trip that Stonewater put together. Three generations of anglers, a father, son, and grandfather, were all fishing with Stonewater out of the same boat when the big bass struck. The two elder gentlemen landed the fish.

93

Get The Point

The guide prefers to use a weedless hook under most conditions. It enables him to get his shiner up in the cover and most of the time, if he doesn't get a fish, he's at least able to get his shiner back out of there. And, he didn't feed the fish that he's trying to catch. With a weedless hook, you're not getting hung up all the time and yanking on the cover, he reasons. That disturbs the fish in it.

"It's not going to be too long before the bass in the cover figures something is going on that's not quite right. She's not dumb," says Stonewater. "Your chances of getting a strike there are becoming less and less."

The hook size should be matched to the size shiner that you're using. That shiner needs to swim as free as it can, and look natural. If you have a big hook hanging out of a little shiner, your chances of catching a big fish are not good. You can trick a bigger bass with a little shiner if you're using light line, a small bobber, and a small hook. The little baitfish will look natural then.

Stonewater uses up to a 7/0 or 8/0 hook with the giant shiners. He makes his own weedless hooks because he hasn't found a large enough or heavy enough factory-made hook to hold the lunker bass. The off-the-shelf hardware was breaking or straightening, so he started to make his own.

"When you're hitting an 11 or 12 pound bass and it's going away from you, that's some impact," says Stonewater. "I've seen rods and reels jerked from people's hands. They just can't believe it."

Current Consideration

In the river currents, Stonewater always hooks his baits through the lips. Even when the shiner tires then, he'll look more natural in the moving water. In a strong current like that found in rivers, the baitfish will wear our quicker, advises Stonewater. It will start dragging sideways in the water. You won't have much chance to catch a big bass then.

In a lake situation where current is not present, an angler can get away with hooking the shiner through the back (dorsal fin area) or near the anal fin, admits Stonewater. Those hooking procedures, though, just won't work as well in current.

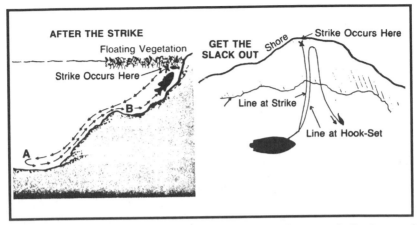

FIGURE 16 - Knowing where the bass is heading and whether or not the line is around an obstacle is very important prior to setting the hook. The largemouth will frequently pin the forage against the bank and strike at point "X". It will then usually move out to deep water to point "A" before returning to its cover-shrouded sanctuary at "B". The line should have little play and be straight between the rod tip and the bass.

Stonewater likes to use 20 to 25 pound test monofilament, but occasionally will go to lighter line and rod for some great action. Regardless, he advises setting the hook quickly. His concerns are the line may drag on something and spook the fish, or the bass may swallow the bait, making it more difficult to release the fish in a healthy state.

Set The Hook

"Just wait until the line is tight, then set", he says. "If the bass has that shiner in its mouth, then the hook is in there too. Her mouth will be closed because she doesn't want the shiner to get out," laughs Stonewater. "You just want to take the time and find out which direction the fish is moving, and then get the slack out. Then you can tighten up and sock it to her."

After the bass takes the bait it will be moving somewhere. It won't just stay put. A largemouth will usually swim straight out to the middle and then turn around and go back under the cover where she was laying. That's a fairly typical pattern for big fish, according to the guide.

The shiner should have enough freedom on the end of your line, Stonewater points out. A big bass will get into the cover and root out the bait.

"The fine line of live bait fishing is handling the rod between the strike and hook set. The proper way to tighten up on the line is to keep the rod tip up at a 45 degree angle from the horizon," he says. "You have better sensitivity in the rod and better feel on what the fish is doing. If you hold it down pointed at the fish, you may get the line too tight and not feel her before you have a chance to set the hook," advises Stonewater. "She'll let go with that increased tension."

By holding the rod tip up, you've got six feet of real "soft" line to play with, according to the guide. The secret of any kind of fishing is being able to feel the fish without it feeling you. The soft line enables an angler to pick up line off the water with less resistance. He can find out easier which way the fish is headed.

"You have time to get turned towards her, get squared away and have your feet planted," says Stonewater. "Then you can really snatch the hook into her. The bass won't even know what happened, except that she ate the wrong shiner!"

Bait Placement

When the shiner is placed along the appropriate bank, Stonewater doesn't move it frequently. He'll check it occasionally to make sure that the shiner hasn't "jumped up" through the weeds and is laying on top of them, out of the water. The bait will do that once in a while to get away from a big bass, but the predator will also tear apart the weeds to get at its prey.

"The shiner should lay there with enough freedom, so that it looks natural," Stonewater says. "That big fish will get into the cover and root out the bait."

The bait must be lively to attract most lunkers, though. The current in a river wears out a shiner quickly, and while two lake fishermen may use three dozen shiners a day, the river anglers could require twice that many.

When a shiner wears down, Stonewater will take it off and put it back in the livewell to recoup a little. The tired baitfish won't regain all its strength, but it will be strong enough for one more trip back into a bass haunt.

When a shiner becomes nervous and struggles in the weeds, yet appears to be hung, the guide will get another bait to that area quickly. Rather than pull that first bait to free it, he'll let it lay. That way, he won't disturb or feed the bass until he gets a second shiner to it.

Hopefully, that second one will be what Stonewater likes to call a "kamikaze" shiner. That's one that will sacrifice itself for a good cause!

CHAPTER 10

DEEP WATER LESSONS

Guide Keys To Prime Bass Locations

"SUSPENDED BASS ARE the hardest to locate," claims Texas bass guide Randy Fite. "They are not as physically active as they are at other times, and they are more difficult to catch!"

"The most difficult time to locate fish, though, is just after the spawn. They move horizontally straight out from the bank, maintaining the same depth," he explains. "They normally remain suspended there until the water below warms up."

As the fish move deeper onto humps and other structure, Fite pulls out his marker buoys and goes to work. He uses several markers to define a ridge and will mark the structure on each break. Markers are dropped some ten to 15 feet away from any fish detected.

If Fite can mark a bass location by precise landmarks, then he usually won't drop markers. If a boat pulls up on his markers while he is fishing, then the guide will often retrieve his buoys. He will then leave if the other boat is not yet positioned.

"If they can't get a reading, it will be rare that the hump-stealing anglers can pull up and catch fish," he contends. "If you know the spot better than they do, you'll always catch more fish."

Fite, of Montgomery, Texas, is one of the most renown depth sounder experts in the country. He has parlayed his structure reading talents and guiding skills into professional bass tournament titles and a technical electronics consulting relationship. Fite feels

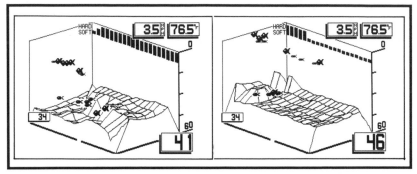

FIGURE 17 - The three-dimensional sonar units now on the market make interpreting the bottom easier for some people. Electronics are your eyes to the bottom, but you must be able to analyze the display information.

that proper installation and operation of the sonar units are keys to his recognition as an expert at locating schools of bass.

Fite is a stickler for details. His locating equipment, wiring and transducer installation and maintenance all receive careful attention. Best performance, according to the pro, should be obtained when the sensitivity is turned up to show a double bottom echo, on either a chart recorder, LCR or flasher, and the noise reject dial is off completely. The speed should be set on high, he advises, for best resolution of bottom structure and fish.

Fite's eyes to the bottom are his electronics, and the correct interpretation of their readings is what finding hump bass is all about. To analyze the readings, knowing the habits of the various fish species is vital.

"Shad generally appear as a large mass, crappie tend to stack vertically," says Fite, "and largemouth usually appear as a group of individual signals related to humps or other structure."

"Knowing which soil types hold fish and how to find them is also extremely important," he adds. "If a third bottom marking appears, for example, hard bottom is present, such as a submerged road bed or highway. If the double bottom tracing disappears completely, the soil is most probably soft."

Another critical analysis technique when looking at the markings is to pay attention to the "V" marks. The more peaked the

Conroe guide Randy Fite is an expert at using electronics to find deep water largemouth habitat.

inverted "V" on a chart recorder, for example, the more directly the transducer is over the fish, according to the guide.

Bass on deep water humps or submerged hill tops are easier to find and catch, Fite contends. He prefers to chase them there, and by deep, I mean deep. I once netted a nice 7 1/2 pound largemouth for him that had taken a jig and eel in 40 feet of water near a submerged hump on a Fayette County Lake.

Fite's favorite locations to find bass depend on the time of the year. During summer and winter, Fite's boat will be found over hilltops and ridges in 20 to 60 feet of water. In the fall, he will check out the upper section of creeks and points in the main part of the lake (8 to 15 feet deep).

Electronic Eyes

During springtime, Fite tries the backs of creeks. He'll pay particular attention to the LCD flasher around the north bank and on main lake flats with depths to seven feet and where cover on the humps is present.

"I'll normally use my electronics to locate the prime hump structure and deep water fish. Then, I will often drop a marker on lakes that I'm not familiar with," he says. "If I know the water well,

Bass often concentrate on deep water humps and a good sonar unit will identify both structure and fish.

I won't drop a marker. The less obvious the bass locations are, the easier it is to keep down the fishing pressure."

Obviously, a successful angler has to locate the fish before he can catch them. I have known a lot of fishermen over the years that could catch bass when placed within casting distance to them. But only a small percentage of anglers can go out and consistently locate the fish. And that is usually 90 percent of the task.

The most important factor in catching largemouth bass is in finding good structure, and submerged humps are hard to beat most of the year. Lure selection and control is important once the fish are located. Not before.

The greatest lure in the tackle box will hook nothing, even during the most skillful presentation ever if there are no bass present. On the other hand, when a large concentration of largemouth are found, it is often possible to catch some of them on a variety of colors and types of lures. Of course, there will usually be an optimal lure selection and presentation to maximize success, but the beginning of productivity is thinking "location."

Anglers known for their guiding activities are usually good at locating the fish. Many are willing to help others learn some of their "secrets" to finding concentrations of bass. Sharing a boat with any of the top guides in the country can be a learning, as well as an extremely pleasurable, experience in bass angling. Most good bass locators use marker buoys, chart recorders and depth flashers for

102

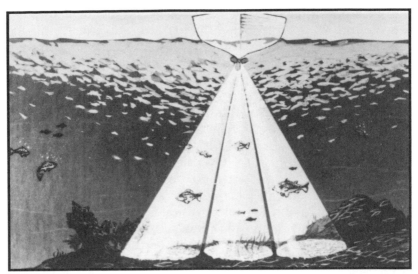

FIGURE 18 - Multiple transducers on some of the newer sonar units help an angler locate fish near the boat. Finding good structure and submerged humps is the key to catching bass from deep water.

their tools, and are highly efficient in the use of their equipment. They normally fish deep humps or other structure, sometimes in eight feet of water and at other times in 20.

Most anglers who fish deep water humps will catch a lot of three to five pound bass. These are the most active and easily caught fish, and they satisfy most fishermen. I have had a couple of dozen trips which resulted in 50 or more bass personally hooked and released. And most were from concentrations on humps in 15 feet or deeper water. To catch such fish, one definitely has to be able to locate them.

Most highly successful anglers use both a chart recorder and flasher (LCD) unit to find bass locations and bass. On mid-lake structures and or unfamiliar waters, they normally use markers. But keeping newly found honey holes secret can be taxing to anyone.

Marker Revelations

I had marked a favorite spot of mine on Fayette County Lake one winter day a few years ago. The spot was a submerged hump in the small power plant cooling reservoir. The surrounding water ranged from 20 to 25 feet, and the pH level was usually optimal (above 7.7) for largemouth around 7 pounds. Outside markers were dropped right at the edge of the sharp incline up to 10 feet on the hilltop that day. The third marker was positioned at the shallowest point on the hump and our boat was anchored nearby.

I sat near the middle one, casting generally toward the curious onlookers in a boat that slowly circled my markers three times. After the last motor-by, the two anglers slowly cruised away, heads still buried in their depth flasher. Over their puttering engine, I overheard one saying, "He has just got to be sitting on something!"

The hump is extremely hard to find since it is right out in the middle of the lake with no nearby natural markers or identification points. It normally takes me ten minutes to locate it and I was fairly sure that, should those structure-swipers return, they wouldn't be able to find it.

In view of the fact that I often caught 25 to 50 bass a day off it, I wanted the hump's exposure to be very limited. I think that dropping the markers in a "deep-shallow-deep" row position will ensure just that. Keeping the better deep water locations secret once your flasher has located a huge school of largemouth bass may be very difficult at times.

Elroy Krueger, a long-time guide on Texas bass waters, burns up a roll or two of graph paper every day in his search for productive hump habitat. He is an expert in relating forage behavior to that of his quarry, the largemouth. Krueger operates his guide service on Chock Canyon Reservoir west of San Antonio. He is also an expert guide on Lakes Calaveras, Braunig, Medina and Canyon.

My biggest bass while fishing with Krueger, a six-pound largemouth, was marked on his chart recorder. The fish was right beside one of Krueger's brush piles located on a hump in 20 feet of water. That's where the guide prefers to find his bass in the depths.

Deeper Trophies

"The giants are deeper," he says. "They'll even spawn in 8 to 12 feet on many area lakes. Seventy-five percent of the eight pound or better bass come from this depth zone."

An isolated submerged stick on a hump in 15 feet of water may harbor lunkers. And Krueger uses a depth recorder to pinpoint such

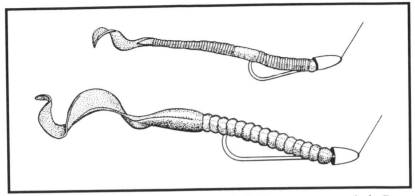

FIGURE 19 - A good deep water worm to work slowly across structures is the Power Worm. It is particularly effective when used in cooler water on inactive largemouth.

spots. His chart recorders are "fine tuned" to expose both baitfish and bass. As the schools of shad move up to shallower water, so will the largemouth, according to Krueger.

Humps and submerged hilltops are favorite Krueger areas of inspection. He'll use a lot of chart paper and drop markers as often as he spies interesting structure and fish. As he finds brush or other good structure on the break in elevation, he tosses out the yellow buoy. While he fishes the marked spots, he'll continue to check out the bottom structure and drop additional markers as determined through new sightings. Krueger contends that he loses one marker buoy almost every day that he's on water. Regardless, he finds the bass.

Krueger opts to search jetties, bridges and dam riprap structure during the cold times. On warm winter days, he checks out the deeper brush piles once the sun has warmed up the water for a few hours. During springtime bass searches, he concentrates on points in eight feet of water. Concrete wall pillars also hold March large-mouths and should be checked out, according to the professional angler.

Most of Krueger's summertime locations are midday spots. Hot weather patterns are brushpile structures in 15 to 20 feet of water and creek channels lying in the same depths. He recommends prime fall check-out locations such as the moss breaks in ten foot depths.

Avoiding & Finding Concentrations

Many of the lakes Krueger fishes around San Antonio and across the state are crowded. He prefers to fish deep structures without the interference of other boats crisscrossing the immediate area. During crowded conditions, he'll search known structure with the chart but without the convenience of marker buoys. Often, he'll triangulate shoreline markers to keep his bass holes secret, but generally Krueger relies on his expert interpretation of the recorder's readout to put fish in the boat.

Success at locating concentrations of bass normally includes knowledge that deep water must be present nearby. Look in depths of 8 to 25 feet for schools of good fish. Check out thoroughly all changes in elevation where cover is present. Brush or rocks in a submerged slough or ditch usually hold bass.

One of my favorite areas to seek the quarry is submerged creeks having a ridge or "flat." These areas provide bass with a holding place where shad will frequently cruise. Bass will hold on ambush points that are along routes followed by shad.

Find the creek channels or depressions that bait fish move along, and you will find the bass. Check out any breaks in a weed line or a tree line. A slough winding up to a submerged road where shad migrate is a favorite spot to find largemouth concentrations. I'll take a Norman Deep Big N and try to crank a few from the prime structure. It usually works.

Post spawn conditions are toughest for most anglers to locate bass. The two or three week transition phase between the spawn and late spring produces a lot of large fish which are generally caught midday. Bread and butter size fish, however, are usually taken in the morning once the bass settle down to more predictable behavior.

May and June fish are generally the easiest to pin down to a location. The most difficult months for most anglers are probably December and January, due to the fronts coming in one after another. The fish are not very active as the water temperature falls.

Noontime is generally an active time for these deep water bass, but the angler has to be looking for only a slight resistance and not a strong tap. That's because the bass may be in a zone of low oxygen content and high pH levels. A Texas-rigged Berkley Power Worm has been highly productive for me under these conditions.

I'll spend a lot of time in areas of heavy structure to thoroughly check out any bass present. A variety of lures are normally thrown to find big schools of fish. If dots on the Lowrance X-5 reveal fish, I will often cast the spot for 15 or 20 minutes. If there are no fish on the flasher or the X-16 chart, I'll seldom waste casts.

Successful guides and their clientele keep their lures in the productive zone, because that is the key to success in finding fish. To join the select group of consistent producers, remember that deep waters may be the best place to locate some big bass.

CHAPTER 11

HOT WATER POINTERS

Summer Heat, Summer Humps

HOT WEATHER NORMALLY makes for an exceptional fishing period on impoundments. Bass are moving deeper into their summer patterns where a good fisherman can frequently locate and catch them. Consistent behavior is the key to improved catches by summertime anglers who work the depths with their deep water arsenal.

Waters like Lake Chickamauga, near Chattanooga, Tennessee, are representative of what an angler might find. Deep water structure fishing can be exceptional then, according to professional guide Mike Bartlett. An average catch of 50 to 100 bass from humps along the lake bottom are frequent. The largemouth ranging from 1 to 2 pounds are "stacked up" on the structure that typically lies in 15 to 18 feet of water.

"Do-nothing" worms, crankbaits and hollow grubs are most effective for large numbers of bass," says Bartlett. "To locate a large fish under such conditions, the angler should rely on a big crankbait."

"You have to check most every hump to determine which one has the better fish on it," he continues. "In the spring, spinnerbaits will attract a lot of 6 to 8 pound bass on the shallow spawning flats. Clear water is usually better for finding large concentrations of fish. If the back of the coves are muddy, just move to the edge of the mud line, and you'll generally find the bass in that area.

My wife, Lilliam, and I journeyed to beautiful Chattanooga one June to fish with Bartlett, and we found that his claims were not exaggerated. I had fished those waters 3 or 4 times previously and had always caught several largemouth. The lake seemed full of them, but the timing had been later in the year when the schools of fish were chasing shad and sticking to the points of the lake's abundant vegetation.

In June, the deep fish in Chickamauga are on the submerged hills, creek banks and ridges. And they are hitting voraciously. With Bartlett, we fished a submerged hump on a point between the confluence of a creek and the main river channel. The point tapered down to 25 feet deep until it merged into a brushy hump that rose to just 15 feet below the surface.

The spot was ideal for summer bass. The nearby creek and river beds were about 35 feet deep, and the largemouth apparently moved along the point to the hump to feed. Our boat was positioned over 25 feet of water and the Carolina worm rigs employed. We cast them about 70 feet to sink at the far edge of the hump.

It didn't take long for action. Lilliam and I had doubles on our second cast, and the bass continued to strike the rest of the morning. The fish were small, between 1 and 3 1/2 pounds, but were they aggressive. We caught and released close to 40 in just a few hours, most from that one hump.

Bartlett has six such humps located around the lake, and all produce bass for the guide. The Chickamauga largemouth normally move onto the humps in late April, but by the end of June the often well-known humps have been pounded by Chattanooga anglers. During late summer, the fishing on the humps there slows.

On other similar waters around the country which may have less fishing pressure, the productive deep water action may last all summer. Many reservoirs, both large and small, produce fish for those that take the time to locate the deep structure. Bass haunts then are those that provide some form of protection, an opportunity for nearby feeding and good access routes to shallow and deep waters. Anglers have to pull themselves away from the shallow emergent cover, though, for maximum benefit.

Tube-Type Grubs

Bartlett, who has been bass fishing for 15 years, likes to toss plastic grubs into the depths. He used the baits to win the 1989

Deep humps often hold trophy-size largemouth. The author caught this 10 pounder on a tube-type lure.

Hungry Fisherman tournament and over $20,000 in cash and prizes. His 37-pound stringer topped a field of 308 anglers on Lake Chickamauga and was a beefy two-day catch on waters known for their abundance of one to three pound largemouth. He culled from 35 bass each day to his tournament limit of 8 fish. That was deep water spring fishing, but the guide normally fishes deep in all kinds of weather.

"Submerged ditches and roadbeds where there are dropoffs and ledges are good spots," says the Chickamauga guide. "Bends in the old river channel often have deep bass, and they aren't as affected by hot summer temperatures as are the shallower fish. Deeper fish in the summer are more concentrated and they average larger sizes. They are just better quality fish."

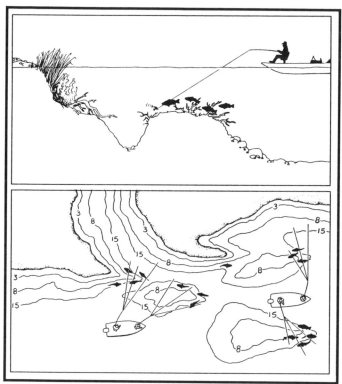

FIGURE 20 - Bass often move to relatively deep water during warm weather. Look for them on humps and points in 8 to 15 feet of water. That's where concentrations of largemouth should exist.

Bartlett utilizes his lake maps and graph recorder to mine the deep concentrations of largemouth. The guide from the home of the Chattanooga Choo Choo often jigs his tube grubs over the fish, once his boat is positioned right above the concentration. If the fish are right off the bottom, he'll place his lures right on top of them. If the bass are suspended at 20 feet in 30 feet of water, he'll try to keep his baits at that level.

Small Impoundments

On a small impoundment last June, I was guiding a man from Iowa. We started the morning fishing near shore. Five bass averag-

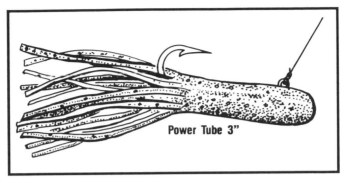

FIGURE 21 - Tube-type grubs are productive in deep waters during the summer months. Position the boat above the fish and jig vertically.

ing two pounds each were pleasing enough action for one hour's work. Our casts to the shoreline cover were fairly productive. However, I knew the waters contained larger bass. Small, injured-minnow plugs were enticing the yearlings from the brush and shallow weed perimeter, but it was time to go after the deeper ones.

Choosing between wormin' the drops or casting a deep-running crankbait to the submerged bars can be difficult. I often opt for a plug initially. Selecting a deep-running Norman DD-22 in a Tennessee shad-finish, I moved the boat to the first drop. The chart recorder printed a gradual slope down 10 feet, then the moving paper denoted a slight bar of two feet stretching for 10 feet or so before the bottom plunged to 20 feet.

Inverted "V's" appeared on the chart paper, and I quietly moved the boat a few yards to capitalize on the discovery. Casts over the hump 50 feet away placed the lures at the right location. Bass awaited 14 feet down. My first three casts resulted in largemouth. A small bass and two pushing four pounds each were released. My Iowa partner hooked two bass, and I had two empty retrieves before another brought two strikes. The second fish was hooked and set the stage for some great structure fishing on that small man-made impoundment.

Casts to the bar met with a 25 percent success ratio. Another ten bass were caught and released on the DD-22, as their average size dropped to about 13 inches. The action was there, but the couple of nice-sized bass taken early were not indicative of the rest of the

113

population. I was looking for a school of concentrated bass of respectable size.

We looked over more bottom and tried two more areas before encountering another productive shelf. The water on each side was 20 feet deep but the hungry largemouth on this structure were in seven feet of water. Six casts in succession produced small bass. The small size was very consistent and many did not exceed 12 inches. We caught another 12 of the battlers in about 10 minutes before moving on.

Finally, I found what I was looking for. A 12-foot ridge with waters on each side dropping to 20 feet was perfect. The old excavated bottom had scattered brush which grew along the ridge before it was inundated. A school of bass also inhabited the area, and our crankbaits moved past the submerged cover only four times before attracting a "pupil."

The fat four pounder leaped skyward twice during the struggle before being relieved of the treble-hook lip lock and returned back to the water. With my boat positioned above the ridge, we cast and retrieved along the structure's entire length.

Over the next hour, we hauled in 28 largemouth that weighed between three and nine pounds. We returned all but one immediately after each battle. Small water bass populations are somewhat fragile, and efforts to maintain the quality fishery that many have requires a conservation-minded angler.

The cooperation of most successful fishermen is needed, since releasing the majority of the bass regardless of size will ensure their future and your success. While the unproductive anglers pose little threat to the bass population in a small body of water, the efficient deep water lure tossers need to become more release-oriented. A small lake can be easily "cleaned out" of bass by just a few good anglers, hurting our chance to come back for some more good action.

Dead Waters

I have often fished small impoundments during the summer when they were supposedly "dead." Even after many spring fishermen had kept entire limits of bass and abused a small water resource,

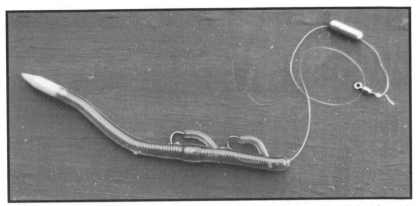

Carolina-rigged worms are productive on deep humps in hot weather. Fish either side of bars to locate the concentrations of bass.

some bass can still be found. Although one lake was reportedly "wiped out," I decided to try it anyway knowing that most anglers even in hot weather are visible-cover pluggers. I found a couple of bottom dropoffs away from the shoreline in relatively deeper water.

My first two stops on a 15-foot deep ridge resulted in approximately 150 unproductive casts and two tight lines. The 13 and 15-inch largemouth were released, and I moved to another ridge in ten feet of water. Small hungry bass were there, and I caught 22 of the 12 to 14-inch fish before leaving. Several times I had two, three or four consecutive strikes and battling largemouth to land.

Such action on summer bass over the years has afforded me the opportunity to catch and release thousands of smaller fish, so I prefer to go specifically after bigger ones. I still appreciate medium-size bass that retreat to the deeper waters and remain actively feeding during hot summer months. The depths may average 10 to 25 feet in the best areas. Deep submerged rock piles and humps are locations of super fishing for all sizes of bass.

When exposed to an impoundment for the first time, several options exist regarding your finding summer bass concentrations. Many terrain variations cry out for your casts, yet some are not conducive to holding your quarry. Areas with abundant brush are more inviting to forage and, correspondingly, to bass. The better angling often lies where one can only look with the chart recorder.

Texas-rigged worms can produce bass that have relocated to deep waters during hot weather. Move off the banks and check out the submerged offshore structure.

I'll generally fish all points, humps, heavy brush areas and submerged extensions to rows or points. If the bass are not in eight feet of water, I'll move to cast deeper spots. Use of a depth finder is often required to find bass, and my units give me a great view of the bottom structure. Lake System's Multi-C-Lector is just as valuable as the depth finder. The unit provides easy to read information on pH, water temperature, clarity, and depth. All the information is valuable to me in finding bass.

Select the lure based on depth, clarity and forage available for maximum action. Locate a summer bass concentration on a hump away from the shoreline that attracts most anglers, and you'll have a chance at a trophy bass and keeping that spot to yourself. In most lakes, there are locations where one can do that!

116

CHAPTER 12

COLD WATER POINTERS

Plans For Winter Success

"ONE WAY TO CATCH fish in the winter months on Truman Lake, where I live, is to use the flutter spoons," claims bass guide Denny Brauer. "I'll work the little side pockets next to the river channel and catch the fish that move up into the cuts. Just throw the flutter spoon out there and basically count it down. A lot of fish will be suspended near the bottom and ready to hit the spoon."

Brauer has caught hot-weather bass off the bottom in waters 55 feet deep. In cold weather, he has taken largemouth from 40 feet deep by vertical jigging. The water is extremely clear at this time of the year, so the pro will spool up with light line and get right over the fish. He'll opt for six to eight pound test monofilament.

Another cold weather ploy of Brauer's is to use the jigging spoons beside bridge pilings. The bass are often very deep suspended underneath schools of shad. Lots of deep water anglers use a Hopkins Spoon or a compact CC Spoon. The successful jigging spoon fishermen just put in their time. They'll get out there and jig. Others change to a flutter spoon and start pumping it through the fish and let it flutter back down to the bottom.

"On strictly suspended bass, it's the difference between night and day," say Brauer. "If I have located tight fish, tight to cover, I've got to drop a straight jigging spoon down on them. But if I have located suspended fish and can't get over the top of them, or get them to hit what I feel is fast enough, I'm going to try the flutter spoon."

"A plastic tube lure is effective on deep cold water bass," he adds, "if it is fished just above them. If you're fishing the bait underneath the fish at this time of year, you'll seldom get a bite. But, when you're fishing above them, they'll come up and get that bait just about every time."

Brauer generally doesn't have too many problems catching bass in the cooler months of January, February, and March. The Camdenton, Missouri, guide admits that the productive deep water techniques that catch winter bass vary from lake to lake. Many methods are not even consistent on one body of water.

"If you want consistent fishing in the Ozarks during the cold water months, you go down to Table Rock Lake or Bull Shoals Lake," says Brauer. "Table Rock is probably my favorite place during those cold water months. In fact, it has a lot of long bars that run well out into the lake."

"To catch bass, you position the boat over the bars and turn on your chart recorder or LCR," he explains. "You need to locate the balls of shad on your electronics. You'll find big swarms of shad suspended on those deep water points, and the bass will be underneath them."

"You're not hunting for fish, you're just hunting for those bait fish," Brauer continues. "Get over the top of them, and you can fish vertical with a tube lure, or a jigging spoon. Those are just a couple of different baits you can catch them on. A lot of the fish are Kentucky bass, and a lot of them are large mouth."

Frontal Problems

How do fronts affect deep water fishing? Not as much as you may think at that time of the year, according to Brauer. There are several fronts that continuously move through the middle part of the country, so the fish are often suspended to start with. They'll be relating to bait fish in most cases.

Fronts then won't affect the bass as they do other times, such as two months later or two months earlier in the season. Later, when bass start to move shallow and prepare to spawn, a front might possibly make them back off. They may hide in cover and stop feeding all together.

"All fronts affect bass to a certain degree and are different," says Brauer. "Fronts are always a negative. In the winter time, some of

Cold weather and deep water fishing are compatible, according to many guides. Fishing in the depths requires the proper tools and knowledge to find and catch bass.

the best fishing I've had occurred as major fronts were moving in or moving through. I always look at winter time fishing as fairly negative anyway. It's going to be fairly slow. We have occasional days where it is good, but overall, it's hard to produce."

The majority of bass that Brauer fishes in the winter are suspended before a front ever hits. There's not a lot of movement with those fish, but once in a while, the front may change the depth of the fish and push them a little deeper. For example, if bass are suspended in 25 foot of water, the front may push them down to 30 foot. If the fish are fairly tight to the point or a drop, the front may either push them out away from the structure more or move them tighter to it.

Wintertime patterns on deep water bass are usually fairly stable. If the water's already cold, the presentation should be very slow anyway, but after a front, you may have to slow the lures down even more. The front may influence the position of the bait more than the bass in many cases.

Fronts also have a less severe effect on deep water bass than they do on those in shallow water. The strike zone may be diminished, however. After a front, shallow bass, in particular, will probably move in tight to cover and have less of a tendency to chase after a bait

"Two things to think about with the deep water winter fish, however, is that their strike zone is not large anyway and secondly, they are already where they want to be," explains former Lake

Tenkiller guide and known TV show host Jimmy Houston. "They don't have to adjust much, but to catch several of them, the bass should be feeding."

Cool Coverage

"You would be surprised how quickly you can cover a mile of submerged creek bed when fishing 35 feet deep," says Houston. "The fish won't be located both on the bank and down on the bottom of the channel, but when you find bass, it'll be a concentration. At that depth, bass just won't be scattered up and down a creek like they normally are in shallow water."

"Once you find that one submerged tree or bush that keeps the bass there, then you can catch a bunch of them," he continues. "In order to catch deep water bass like that, though, the lake should have a healthy fishery. If you can't catch many fish from the shallows at other times of the year, you won't be able to catch many winter fish in the deep either."

The problem, according to Houston, is that there aren't many fish in some bodies of water, and in order to successfully fish the depths, you should concentrate on lakes which have large numbers of bass in them. Toledo Bend and Sam Rayburn in Texas, and West Point in Georgia, are three examples. Many places just don't have a sufficient number of bass in them for the deep water angler to be successful.

Bass in extremely clear lakes, like Bull Shoals in Arkansas, may move very deep in the winter, according to the affable Oklahoman. The topography of a clear water lake in the mountains, like Oklahoma's Tenkiller or Missouri's Table Rock, is normally composed of quick-sloping rock bluffs. There is very little vegetation in those lakes, so Houston concentrates on fishing water 14 to 19 feet deep during the winter months.

Fish in these types of lakes normally relate to very steep bluffs and the sheer drops that form a point near major creek or river channels. In the colder water, Houston's boat will be positioned over such spots, where he'll opt for either a jig and eel or a big spinnerbait. When after the deep winter bass, he'll fish both lures extremely slow.

A heavy jigging spoon can cover deeper water faster than any other lure or live bait, and when fished vertically, is extremely accurate.

The jig size that the TV show host selects depends on the depth he is fishing. Houston will use a 1/4 ounce jig down to about 14 feet and then switch to a 1/2 or 5/8 ounce jig for deeper waters. He prefers the larger types of eels behind the jig head during the winter. Big bass love such fare, he reports.

Larger fish, fortunately, are more accessible in the winter, but they may only feed once every six days or so. It's difficult to make sure that your lure is in their vicinity when they are feeding. Smaller fish may eat every day, but in the winter, for some reason, they aren't readily caught. You may go out in the winter time and get six bites, according to Houston, but they may all be over four pounds.

A flatland lake, like Sam Rayburn, has lots of vegetation and that is the key there to bass location in the winter. Even in a shallower, highly vegetated lake, the bass are still usually holding on the steeper edges. Those edges then are not rock bluffs, but moss. They form sharp edges at the point where the vegetation terminates, and the bass relate to such just like they would a bluff, according to Houston.

Patience is a definite factor in the success of deep water bass fishing. An angler may go four hours without the first strike, and then get 30 strikes in the following 40 minutes. It's like that in the deep.

Bottom Structure

"In similar lakes without the vegetation, I concentrate on the banks of the submerged creek channels," says Houston. "I like to find creeks with 40 to 50-foot bottoms, because they'll have 25 to 30-foot deep banks. The bass will normally be on those banks, and that's when I like to fish spoons for them."

Houston, who grew up fishing deep water structures, is a fanatic about the use of marker buoys. He'll normally mark the creek channels with his buoys and start fishing his jigging spoons in the creek itself. He'll toss his spoon out along the path between buoys checking out both the channel and the banks, particularly those bends.

When trying to locate bass, his casts cover more water and are, therefore, more efficient. He'll fish the spoon back to the boat, just as he would a plastic worm. Hangups are inevitable with such a technique. In lakes with heavy timber, Houston acknowledges that you have to be very careful about the retrieve.

"When a lot of new spoon fishermen feel resistance, they set the hook," cautions Houston, "but you can't do that if you are casting the spoon out and jerking it back to the boat. You'll go through a lot of spoons if you do. You have to have a sensitive touch to realize what is brush and what is a fish."

The Oklahoma bassman prefers to throw a 3/4 or 1 ounce jigging spoon onto the bank at a bend and then work it off and into the creek channel. Once the bass are located, he'll mark the spot with a buoy and jig the spoon right over them. Most good deep water fishermen agree with Houston that jigging is the best way to put those fish in the boat.

Jigging spoons are effective on bass that are hungry, as well as those that may just be in the "line of retrieve." Occasionally, the spoon will snag a bass on the outside of its mouth, and after that and the ensuing battle has occurred, others in the school may be excited and may get inspired to start feeding. Houston has found that a seemingly-dormant concentration can be "motivated" to become active.

In the winter, fish slow, and the friction on the other end of the line should make up for the harsh weather above.

CHAPTER 13

TOUGH TIME REPORTS

Frontal Suggestions For Sluggish Bass

LOCK-JAW BASS after a blue-norther' pose particular problems that many anglers seldom overcome, but there are ways to approach those conditions and solve them. Technique, location and equipment considerations are many, but Texas guides Randy Fite and Zell Rowland can normally figure out the productive ways.

Both men guide on Lake Conroe and other Central Texas waters and have experienced more than their share of tough frontal conditions. Each, in his own way, has learned to combat them. When a 'blue norther' blows through leaving clear skies and cold northerly winds, these men are experienced enough to consider other variables before establishing a game plan.

The type of lake that you're situated on is very important, for example. If it has depth and if the fish can go deep, most successful anglers would then fish the deeper bass, if the winds would allow them to get out on the open water.

"Under these conditions, you have to really sit on those spots," says Fite. "You'll work a lot harder for each individual fish that you're going to catch. I would just slow myself down and really concentrate. I would work each area harder and expect to catch less fish."

"You have to keep one thing in mind, though," he cautions. "The fish are not going to be aggressive. If you have a few spots that you hit under good conditions, and you don't get a bite within 15 minutes, you pick up and leave."

Fite will generally fish the edge of a creek bank on Conroe or Fayette County when a cold front moves through. If he's on a lake with numerous shallow (five to 10 foot) fish when the cold front hits, he searches for a big moss bed that might come up in 20 feet of water. Finding such would allow him to flip under those type of conditions. Fite's main bait would then be a jigging eel, and he would simply move his boat along slowly and fish the deeper line of moss.

"The fish would probably be in a pre-spawn type of situation in February, and the one thing to look for at this time of year is a warming trend," says Fite. "If you have three or four days of nice weather, and then a cold front sets in, the fish want to be fairly close to where they're actually going to move on to spawn. The backs of creeks and some secondary-type creek situation are areas that you want to be fishing," he says.

Secondary Creeks

"When the cold front has blown through, I would suspect that those fish would tend to back off into a creek," says Fite. "On most reservoirs, I would fish at the back end of a major creek or part of a secondary creek that's connected to a flat area which would be the final spawning grounds."

"I would fish that creek right where it connected with the flat area and I would fish the lip of the creek itself. The fish would normally back off the flat into the creek if they had already moved up to begin bedding," he explains. "And again, I would probably fish a slow moving bait, such as a jigging eel."

Rowland would likewise fish a jigging spoon or a jig-and-eel type bait under such cold water conditions. He prefers something to work either right in front of the bass, like a spoon, or something like the jig and eel that's worked very, very slow.

"You just have to spend a lot more time and effort catching each individual fish, and on each spot that you're fishing," he says. "More so than you would on a day when the fish are more aggressive and active."

Most anglers are going to look for the same thing during such conditions, which would be a cove or a calm spot to get out of the wind. In February, you will usually find fish in most southern lakes on a creek bank somewhere, Rowland believes. And when you do

During a front, guide Randy Fite will warm up with a big bass. He'll often spoon one up from the depths.

find them at that location during this time of the year, he feels that a cold front would not move the bass.

Two Strike Projections

"If they're on a creek bank, the front will simply slow down their habit of feeding," he says. "You just have to sit there and more or less keep chucking, knowing that if you get 20 strikes the day prior to the front, you may only get five the day after."

Rowland faced the toughest conditions of his fishing career in February of 1982, when a norther' was blowing through the Lake Conroe area. Winds of 35-40 miles an hour aided a temperature drop of from 50 degrees to about eight. It was the most miserable conditions that he ever fished, according to the guide.

"I had to slow myself down on the water that I was used to fishing," he says. "I've been guiding and fishing there for 13 years, and I could pull into an area knowing there were fish there. I was catching my fish on the edge of a moss line, but the fish were real inactive."

Rowland fished for one or two strikes each day and claims to be fortunate in finding some fish that were slow, but active. He had to work an area for an hour or so before finally getting a strike. The fish that he caught ranged from four to five pounds.

Fite, who has faced some extremely tough conditions, calls a cold front and muddy, cold water the worst.

"If the water temperature is low, and the water is muddy, you can almost forget catching fish with any consistency whatsoever," Fite points out. "Under such conditions, the only bait that I would normally fish is a worm. The key to success would be working it as slowly as possible."

In deep cold water, anglers often hop the lure, but bass may not strike it. After frontal conditions, you may have to work the worm extremely slow. The fish are almost always sluggish in extremely cold water conditions.

Worm Fare

"The plastic worm is probably the most versatile lure under such conditions," says Fite. "But there are times when the worm is not the best type of lure to throw, and that is whenever the fish have not been too affected by the front and are still aggressive. There are other baits that can cover more water, and therefore catch more fish."

"But day in and day out, the plastic worm is probably more suited for a wide variety of fishing conditions and water than any other lure," he says. "There is no one lure that can be relied on at all times because of the variables that must be taken into consideration, but I like the plastic worm."

"Under most frontal conditions, you may want to select a bait that you can cover a lot of water with," adds Rowland. "When the fishing is tough, you have to go searching for different types of lures. In a four hour period, you can cover a great deal of them."

On post-frontal days, you'll seldom find active fish, but occasionally bass may get active. It may be for only 20 minutes, depending on the other weather conditions present, according to the Conroe guide. He would normally cover a great deal of water searching for a producing-type of pattern.

The plastic worm is probably the most versatile lure under tough conditions. That is particularly true after a cold front has turned bass inactive.

"The plastic worm is probably the biggest fish-catching type bait on the market, whether before or after the front," says Rowland. "But in my opinion, to fish a worm properly you should never fish a worm fast. Therefore, since you cannot cover a great deal of water with the worm, my bait selection under some tough frontal conditions would be either a crankbait or some type of top water bait."

If you can't catch bass with the slow approach, you may have to alter your strategy or technique to salvage the day and put a few fish in the live well. If the conditions are right for the slow-presented lure and the fish aren't biting, Fite would definitely change his pattern.

Learning From Zero Strikes

"Whatever I had been doing that morning, I would do something different that afternoon," he says. "I think many people have difficulty with changing."

To combat difficult fishing conditions, many guides turn to the plastic worm and fish it very slow.

"If I fish four hours and have not had a strike, it doesn't mean that I've necessarily had a bad day or wasted time," Fite explains. "All I've been doing is getting that much closer to the bass and, in the next four hours, I may catch 20 fish."

"I've used those four hours to eliminate something which I felt might have been good," he continues. "Now I should have a good idea of what is holding the fish. That time spent is productive, if you're fishing in a systematic method. If you just go out and randomly cast the water for four hours without catching a fish, you don't know any more than you did when you started that morning."

"If you bounce back and forth, fishing here and there," says the guide, "you have gained little 'new' information. But, if you take those four hours to eliminate something and didn't catch a fish, then you have a good idea of what else you can try to catch fish, another type of pattern for example."

"As long as you're fishing in a systematic method and not catching fish, that only means that you're getting that much closer to figuring out how to catch them," explains Fite. "People just don't realize that they're not fishing in any kind of system, so they're not really accomplishing much while on the water. At the end of the day, if they haven't caught a bass, they haven't learned anything. They are no closer to figuring out what's going on in the lake."

The one thing that Fite can usually rely on under tough frontal conditions is his flippin' stick. The long rod is preferred by many anglers because, generally, if conditions are tough, they're trying to find scattered fish. When the fish are in very dense cover, guides like Fite and Rowland use a flippin' stick in order to present the lure quietly to the fish.

"I'll use a flippin' stick for the simple reason that I can cover a lot more water with it and present the bait ten times better than if I was just taking a regular casting rod and running down the bank," says Rowland. "You have to present the bait from a position where you can flip it into a bush."

Hopefully, that bait will be right by the nose of a bass every time. When it's cold, though, the successful angler will adapt to the conditions at hand. Productive techniques are not secret. When the weather changes, so must you.

To cope with frontal weather conditions has always been a challenge for most bass anglers. Discovering the most effective patterns during such inclement weather, though, will help catch fish. Those that do formulate a successful 'game plan' will find great rewards!

CHAPTER 14

STORMY GUIDANCE

Strategies For Wind And Rain

LIGHTNING CRACKED around them as torrential rains moved through the area preceding a front. Guide Bud Pruitt and his client, however, were staying relatively dry and having the time of their lives. The two were catching bass on about every tenth cast.

They had arrived at Sam Rayburn early that morning, before the rains had started. It wasn't long, though, before the wind came up and the squall approached. Other boats scurried for cover on the banks as Pruitt and his partner watched the clouds closely.

They were located over a submerged hydrilla bed when the skies really opened up all around them. It was pouring rain a few hundred yards away from both sides of Pruitt's boat, and the thunder and lightning continued at a distance, yet they remained relatively dry. It seemed as though every bass in that part of the lake wanted to feed in, around, and over that hydrilla.

Largemouth were eager for any topwater lure and would "blow up" on buzz baits and other surface fare that the two anglers offered. The fish were especially interested in the bait as it was being quickly retrieved. The action on the 1/8 ounce buzzers above holes in the weedbed was heart-stopping at times, according to Pruitt.

The chartreuse lures made a small chirping noise as they scooted across the surface and the bass explosions should have consumed the two anglers' attention. They didn't however. The young professional guide from Houston, Texas, watched the storm close in on either side of them.

"It was a monumental experience," says Pruitt. "The fishing was just too good and we didn't want to leave. We sat right there in the middle of the lake, the only boat out there, rain pouring on either side of us, and killed the bass on little yellow buzz baits."

Finally, the fall storm broke and the skies cleared. The red-hot fishing also continued, and the twosome caught bass until dark that day. The larger bass were taken nearer the bottom by fishing baits down through the grass, while the active fish on top usually ran smaller. The two anglers caught and released over 100 largemouth from 10 inches to 3 1/2 pounds that stormy day and didn't even get wet. For Pruitt, who fishes over 100 days each year, that stormy day was memorable, but it was one of many he has faced.

Unpredictable Rainfall And pH

November weather can be unpredictable, and 'northers' may frequently blow through an area. Fronts don't have to scare an angler if he learns to safely reap its benefits -- the good fishing. The tail end of the good weather and the time just as the front passes can be productive. An approaching front with rain but little wind might trigger a feeding spree that can last several hours.

Usually, after the clouds and rain have blown through leaving clear blue skies, the fisherman can hang up his rods, because very few fish will be caught. The severity of the front determines whether there is any hope at all for catching a couple of bass. A frigid front will cool water temperatures quickly and slow the fish's metabolism (and feeding movements).

Bass may also be driven deeper by heavy rainfall, which lowers the lake's pH values to intolerable levels. Values of pH between 6.5 and 8.5 are suitable for finding some feeding bass. High winds accompanying the rains may, through wave action, mix the pH and make the values similar from top to bottom. The stronger the wind, the deeper the mix will take place. For example, if the pH is high near the surface and low near the bottom, the windward shore should offer a moderate pH from top to bottom.

If the surface is more turbulent and roily over a period of time, it will prevent light from penetrating the water as deep as the submergent plant growth. With plant photosynthesis activity down, the result might be a lower pH in that area. Photosynthesis increases

The author doesn't mind a heavy cloud bank and impending storm when he's bass fishing. Damp, misty days during the fall can mean an opportunity to tangle with hungry bass.

pH levels in the immediate vicinity of vegetation, and on most lakes, that's vital for the plant growth to hold bass during the fall.

"A shallow pH cline or thermocline, commonly found in the fall, could be completely wiped out by high winds," says Joe Meirick, CEO at Lake Systems Division. "During the hotter times of the year, the clines are normally found a lot deeper in Texas lakes. You won't find storms then that mix the waters enough to destroy those breaklines. The breaklines will be there and the bass will be concentrated above them."

"As the wind comes up and the surface becomes rougher, you won't see as much light penetration," adds the developer of the pH Monitor and Color-C-Lector. "That will cause fish to strike different-colored baits. Winds over an extended period could affect pH levels, depending on the strength of the wind and the vegetation below the surface."

Storm Colors

Former fisheries biologist, Bob Knopf, believes that line color is also an important angling consideration when fishing in stormy weather. A more fluorescent line will enable an angler to see the point where the line is entering the water. With a bow whipping about, that's not an easy task in high winds and over choppy surface waters.

"The water is busted up underneath too, so the fluorescents aren't as visible there," Knopf points out. "You just have more control when you can easily watch the line. You'll catch more fish as a line watcher."

A line like Photochromic TriMax is ideal for such a situation. It has the hi-vis fluorescent blue above the water yet almost disappears beneath the surface. Berkley has been able to develop the line with a smaller particle pigment while maintaining the above-water fluorescent characteristic. As the light diminishes underwater, wavelengths of light are lost and the special Photochromic pigments drop out more quickly than those in conventional fluorescent lines.

Wind Disturbances

Stormy weather and high winds that move anglers to protected shores may have other benefits. Dislodged plankton and small crustacean are suspended in the roily waters, attracting small forage fish. Bass usually move to wind-blown, turbid waters for the feast. Actively feeding bass in prime areas such as along windward points and irregular shorelines are there for the angler, if he can fish those areas.

Keeping the boat from being blown to shore is the main consideration when fishing a windward location. Smart anglers will lower the bow-mounted electric motor to its maximum extension. That

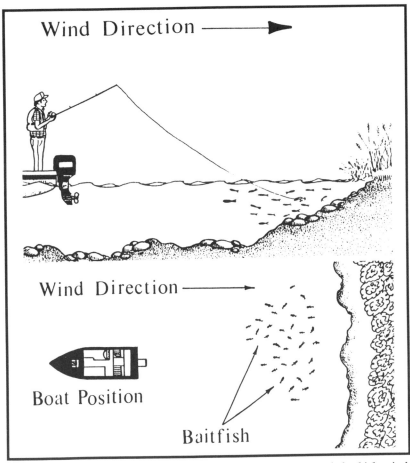

Wind Direction

Wind Direction

Boat Position

Baitfish

FIGURE 22 - *Bass feed actively with an approaching front and the high winds associated with it. Baitfish are pushed to the windward shore where bass will often congregate also.*

will help keep the prop below the surface of the water when the bow is forced up by the high waves. The fisherman should also use the foot control (if the motor has one) from a seated position. That allows maximum control of the boat when it is not safe to be standing in big waves.

If the trolling motor is a 12/24 volt model, he would be wise to put the control on 24 volts and maintain constant power at a low-speed operation while quartering into the wind. In that way, the boat is under maximum control, and when additional instantaneous power is required, the motor can be easily "throttled-up."

Finally, throw a fast-moving bait such as a crankbait or spinnerbait along a windward shore or structure. The bass there are probably active and the boat is moving, so cover ground quickly and find the fish. In rough weather, you'll want to be moving and casting, because that is you best bet to utilize the livewell.

The catching conditions are good in high winds and rain, since the angler can fish closer to the fish due to the limited visibility of the water. Bass will stay in extremely muddy water and will move only when it becomes so muddy that sediments begin collecting in their gills. Such a tremendous storm, however, would probably find most of us off the water.

CHAPTER 15

TIDE AND MOON INDICATIONS

Brackish Water Tricks For Dog Days

MANY ANGLERS ARE TOTALLY unfamiliar with fishing tidal waters. The changes in water level and the salt-water influence into these brackish waters sometimes leaves freshwater anglers confused. However, tide waters are not difficult to fish, and, in fact, most tidal rivers are often more productive in the dog days of summer than are nearby lakes.

Once anglers discover the neglected bass fishery, they will wonder what took them so long to explore the tidal-influenced tributaries. Knowing how to fish these waters is vital to bass angling productivity.

Woo Daves, a guide and professional angler from Chester, Virginia, is very familiar with tidal-influenced waters. He has fished virtually every location east of the Mississippi River. According to him, tactics used on one tidewater body will work, regardless of where you fish. Once you learn the basic successful bass techniques and understand the tide flow, fishing becomes much easier.

"What many fishermen don't realize is that they need to study the tide chart and plan their fishing around the tides," explains Daves. "Tide charts are posted yearly and are good for the whole year. Without any doubt, fishing is always best on the outgoing tides and on the first hour of incoming. After the first hour, as a rule, you might as well pack it in, but only in that spot."

"At this point, tide charts comes in very handy," continues the guide. "The chart will help you determine the direction of the tide, and you can take advantage of it by moving with it. For example, when I fish the Chickahominy River near Richmond, I'll use the tide chart to gain three to four hours of extra fishing during the prime time. It shows that by moving from the mouth of the river towards Richmond, I can always be at the peak tides."

"In other words, go with the flow," Daves adds. "You are catching fish around low tide at point A. When the tide comes in, you can move up river to point B ahead of the incoming tide and still be fishing the good tide. This can go on for a while!"

Many new tide water fishermen, and those who don't understand the tides, will locate fish at one point and continue fishing it after the tide turns. That is not the way to maximize the catch. The fishermen would only have to move up river to points B or C, and they would be fishing a good tide again, according to Daves.

Structural Variety

Tide water rivers offer a large variety of fishing structures that can usually be found by the moving bass angler. Each structure can be effectively fished, although different fishing techniques to optimize productivity may be needed. In moving water, that's always a consideration.

"No matter what part of the country you're fishing, the current and fishing techniques are very important," stresses the Virginian. "Bass react to current and structure in a different pattern, depending on tidal flow, and anglers must know how to approach each situation. For example, vegetation in the form of lily pads is prevalent throughout many tidal waters. But fishing around lily pads is more productive on high tides."

"Clumps of pads next to deep water are the best locations for finding bass then," explains the guide. "If you can catch a high outgoing tide at early morning or late evening, I've found a buzzbait to be most productive."

"Matching the lures to the available forage is of paramount importance," says Daves. "There are a lot of small baitfish working the pads, and that makes small crankbaits very effective in that habitat."

I've found a Norman Little N to be highly effective at luring a good share of largemouth from bonnets and lilies. Casting the crankbaits into the pads and retrieving them very slowly is effective.

140

Woo Daves is familiar with tidal-influenced waters and the overlooked bass they hold. Big largemouth are often neglected by freshwater guides who avoid brackish waters.

Once reeled down to their 'working depth,' crankbaits will come through pad stems fairly well without hanging up.

Many river fishermen will ease their boat right along the edge of the pads and flip worms back into the vegetation. Daves finds such a ploy to his liking and uses the flippin' technique often.

"Don't pass up using a small top water bait along the edge of the pads either," advises Daves. "Two-inch injured minnow lures and tiny surface plugs with spinners fore and aft are favorites."

Piling Strategy

Pilings are also popular bass habitat in tidal waters, and one of Dave's favorite structures in tidal fishing. Fish tend to school in summer and fall on pilings, according to the guide, and he has caught many limits of largemouth from one set of pilings.

"Bass will be facing into the current flow during the tidal flow," says Daves. "You need to fish your lure past the pilings letting it bump the piling as it comes by. Be prepared to set the hook."

"Now, an inexperienced fisherman will make another mistake when fishing tidal water," says Daves. "Matching the right weight lure to the strength of the tidal flow is necessary. Tides flow at different speeds, and it's very important to match the right weight of lure to the current movement."

Mid-tides, those between low and high, seem to flow the fastest, and at that time Daves tries to use heavier lures. Then, as the tides in that particular area slow down, he'll select a lighter lure.

"If you throw a 1/4 ounce lure and the tides are swift, your lure will not get down to the fish," he explains. "They will be deeper, so you need to change to a heavier lure, say 1/2 ounce. By the same token, you need to revert to a lighter lure on slack tides."

One other productive trick to use around pilings in brackish water is to keep three rods rigged with the same size crankbait, according to Daves. Each should have a different lip, however, so you can work shallow, medium and deep waters.

Don't confine your tidal fishing only to pilings though. Other excellent structures are trees, logs and sunken boats that are found throughout most moon-influenced waters.

"Worms work well around this type of submerged structure, explains Daves. "There are three basic colors that I have used successfully to produce large numbers of bass. Motoroil, muddy water violet and black with chartreuse tail are frequently the most popular choices."

The tidal flow strength and appropriate sinker size are also extremely critical, Daves believes.

"On slack tides I'll use a 1/8 ounce weight," he says. "As the tide becomes swifter, I'll work up to a 1/4 ounce or heavier. I'll use whatever it takes to get the worm down into the structure and keep it there."

Effective Presentations

Presentation is most important when fishing the worm in tide water. Daves fishes about 200 days each year and has specific thoughts on the correct presentation to use on tidal-influenced habitat.

"Cast to the structure directly," he points out, "And the current flow will move the worm past the structure before it descends to the

Bass that move with the currents of lunar influence are usually healthy and robust. Seldom will an angler catch a ten pounder in tidal waters, though.

bottom. As a general rule you need to cast at least two to three feet above the submerged structure, letting the current pull your worm or lure into the bass-holding habitat."

Many tidal rivers and basins in the U.S. are bordered by cypress trees. Bass anglers know that these areas are particularly good structure for bass in all waters. In tidal waters, they're excellent bass habitat during the springtime. Daves prefers to fish them by positioning his boat so he can throw past the cypress on the up current

143

side, letting the bait bump the tree on its way downstream.

"Most cypress are located in shallow water and they are close to good spawning areas," explains Daves. "I have found three lures work well in this cover: shallow running crankbaits, spinnerbaits and plastic worms."

Drop Baits

Dropoffs are plentiful near creek mouths, ditches and runoffs. Most offer changes in topography (elevation) around their mouth, and Daves prefers to use a paddletail grub in such locations. Smoke or muddy water violet on a 1/4 or 3/8-ounce head are employed, depending on the current flow.

Daves will cast up onto the shallower part of the structure and bounce the jig and grub off obstructions along the drop. A deep-running crankbait is also productive in these areas and he'll go to one if the grub doesn't attract the interest of a largemouth.

Feeder creeks are basically shallow creeks that attract the bass to feed at high tide and shouldn't be passed up, according to the guide. As the water recedes, the largemouth will move to the edges out of the marsh grass. A very effective method for fishing small feeder creeks is to use the "swimming worm."

"My swimming worm is rigged on a 10-pound leader with a swivel and two #1 hooks on either end," explains Daves. "The hooks put a curve in the worm which creates a "swimming" or rotating effect. A slow steady retrieve should attract a bass strike."

Tidal bass are frequently feistier and require sturdy equipment to insure them reaching the net. Tidal waters also harbor salt-water species that often compete with the bass for the anglers' offerings. Daves prefers to use strong rods and reels.

"I will use 14-pound test line on my reel and sometime a heavier leader," he explains. "This helps avoid a break-off if a saltwater fish with large teeth strikes or if my line scrapes any barnacles."

Tidal angling is a challenging, successful bass catching experience for anglers who study their techniques and the specific estuary environment.

"Pay close attention to the tide chart and current flow," advises Daves. "And match your tackle to meet the appropriate needs."

CHAPTER 16

OBSERVATIONS AROUND YOU

Awareness Leads To More Largemouth

THE GUIDE MOVES his boat through three to four foot deep flats after dark and searches for blind mosquitoes. It's a unique way of finding shallow-water largemouth, but it works.

"The blind mosquitoes are the ones that don't bite," said the old St. Johns River captain. "We'll use a spotlight and check out the various beds of weeds until we find a bunch."

He'll return the following morning to patches of vegetation that hold those specific bugs. At night, he marks the potential bass-feeding spots with a limb-stake so that they are easy to find.

The reason that bass love such spots is obvious. Small forage fish will move in during the night to feed on the mosquitoes. Big bass often follow, according to the man who has caught 10-pound-plus largemouth on both live shiners and artificial baits. In fact, his largest bass were found that way.

A shallow-water tip-off to the presence of big bass was revealed to me by another Lake George guide. He watches the actions of coots, the small weed-eating ducks that often cover those waters in the early spring. They are seemingly everywhere on the miles of vegetated flats around the lake.

"Coot will skirt around a large bass on a bed or at the edge of cover," he told me. "They will actually look at that bass as they pass around her."

The guide watches the coot's eyes as it swims in an arc, apparently moving around a submerged predator. This will often key him

145

because of the current pushing at cattails, resembled others over the eight-foot deep flats. The bass fishing there did not.

Catfish Capers

On Lake Okeechobee, a guide friend and I were chasing schooling largemouth one day and found something interesting. We had started fishing early, and had no strikes after an hour of plugging the dense vegetation. Some "anglers" after another species of fish clued us into the location of the concentration of bass.

A wooden commercial rig about 20 feet long pulled into the grassy Lake Okeechobee cove. The catfishermen were there to run their nets. The men tossed a grappling anchor overboard to snag a heavy rope that secured their net to the bottom. Then, they pulled up a wire net with several catfish flopping within. The three "crackers" selected their prey and dumped the remaining fish back into the lake.

The catfishermen re-baited their net and tossed it overboard. They cranked the outboard and moved down the shoreline toward another net. Few realize the value in following the commercial catfish netters. Bass move into the open areas to feed on the crippled shad and other forage fish that are tossed back from those boats.

We moved toward the "chummed" area. My first cast to the area landed near the net location, and on about the third rotation of my reel's handle, a largemouth sucked in my tail spinner lure. The three and a half pounder hit the lake's surface mad. It burst skyward three times before I could net and release it. A second, quick cast resulted in another strike and I soon landed its twin.

Over the next hour, my guide friend and I switched to crankbaits and continued to work the area where the net had been baited and the majority of its contents dispersed. Another dozen fat largemouth were taken and released. The schoolers never did become active on the surface, but silver-hued, Norman Big N crankbaits accounted for some exciting early action.

The productive angler often has to try something different in order to increase the catch rate. Following catfishermen around is different. Developing methods and expertise at finding and catching the quarry is often very hard work.

Crankbaits were used around the commercial catfish trapping area to produce numerous largemouth.

Habitat Considerations

Hydrilla has spread throughout the country and provides fish with extraordinary cover. Many anglers, though, are bewildered by the mass of weed in their favorite waters. Others, like Orange Springs guide Dan Thurmond, have found unique "bass signs" in such areas. He has caught many of his trophies in the last few years from unique structure.

"When they spray chemicals over the hydrilla to make boat lanes, this will knock the weed down only where they sprayed," he told me. "As the water level rises above the weed mass, there is a slot below the majority of the hydrilla."

"Bass will use these trails to move along because they are one to two feet deeper than the top of the submerged hydrilla," he explained. "The change may be small to detect, but it's definitely worth looking for if you can find it!"

Another guide friend looks for firm sand bottoms with reed growth to find his spring and winter largemouth. A mud or muck bottom is usually void of fish, he contents, so it's important to check out the bottom characteristics around the lake. Some areas will hold big fish, others won't, but the sandier the better.

Create Your Own Hot Spot

Again, the enterprising angler can create his own unique bass catching spots. When running lake tributaries in a boat, position it near shore so that the wake will stir up the water adjacent to the shoreline. The disturbance will also knock small forage into the water and bass will soon be moving along the area to feed. Turn the boat around and then fish the banks with the stained water.

Better yet, do this before dark and come back along the shore after sunset. Using similar reasoning, pick those lakes to fish that are crowded with speed boaters all weekend long and be there on a Sunday night. The boat traffic should keep the shoreline muddy and very productive for bass anglers.

While many anglers thoroughly cover shallow shorelines in search of bass, some head for deep water. They often catch more than their share of bigmouth bass, particularly if they can interpret depth finder readings. Huge concentrations of big bass have been caught by anglers trained to understand the markings of a chart recorder.

In open water, "bass signs" are available via the chart recorder. Activity in deep water, suspended bass or shad can lead to an impressive quantity of quality fish. Once that 'activity depth' has been established, productive anglers will move over to nearby structures that are lying at the same approximate depth.

The chart will help locate active bass that are in a feeding position on structure. During colder weather, you may have to search diligently for fish on the bottom. Sometimes, the largemouth will be laying so close to the bottom that you will have to catch two or three before the remainder will move off enough to show on a recorder. Summer bass are usually six inches to two feet off the bottom and very obvious on sonar equipment.

Regardless of whether you're on a massive lake or a tiny one, look for the unique "bass signs" and try something different to locate and catch them. Develop tricks from your own observations to put a few more fish from any water into the boat.

BASS SERIES LIBRARY!

A Wealth Of Information
For Bass Fishermen

By Larry Larsen

   I. FOLLOW THE FORAGE FOR BETTER BASS ANGLING - VOL-UME 1 BASS/PREY RELATIONSHIP - The most important key to catching bass is finding them in a feeding mood. Knowing the predominant forage, its activity and availability, as well as its location in a body of water will enable an angler to catch more and larger bass. Whether you fish artificial lures or live bait, you will benefit from this book.

SPECIAL FEATURES
o PREDATOR/FORAGE INTERACTION
o BASS FEEDING BEHAVIOR
o UNDERSTANDING BASS FORAGE
o BASS/PREY PREFERENCES
o FORAGE ACTIVITY CHART

II. FOLLOW THE FORAGE FOR BETTER BASS ANGLING - VOLUME 2 TECHNIQUES - Beginners and veterans alike will achieve more success utilizing proven concepts that are based on predator/forage interactions. Understanding the reasons behind lure or bait success will result in highly productive, bass-catching patterns.

SPECIAL FEATURES
> o LURE SELECTION CRITERIA
> o EFFECTIVE PATTERN DEVELOPMENT
> o NEW BASS CATCHING TACTICS
> o FORAGING HABITAT
> o BAIT AND LURE METHODS

III. BASS PRO STRATEGIES - Professional fishermen have opportunities to devote extended amounts of time to analyzing a body of water and planning a productive day on it. They know how changes in pH, water temperature, color and fluctuations affect bass fishing, and they know how to adapt to weather and topographical variations. This book reveals the methods that the country's most successful tournament anglers have employed to catch bass almost every time out. The reader's productivity should improve after spending a few hours with this compilation of techniques!

SPECIAL FEATURES
> o MAPPING & WATER ELIMINATION
> o LOCATE DEEP & SHALLOW BASS
> o BOAT POSITION FACTORS
> o WATER CHEMISTRY INFLUENCES
> o WEATHER EFFECTS
> o TOPOGRAPHICAL TECHNIQUES

IV. BASS LURES - TRICKS & TECHNIQUES - Modifications of lures and development of new baits and techniques continue to keep the fare fresh, and that's important. Bass seem to become "accustomed" to the same artificials and presentations seen over and over again. As a result, they become harder to catch. It's the new approach that again sparks the interest of some largemouth. To that end, this book explores some of the latest ideas for modifying, rigging and using them. The lure modifications, tricks and techniques presented within these covers will work anywhere in the country.

SPECIAL FEATURES
> o UNIQUE LURE MODIFICATIONS
> o IN-DEPTH VARIABLE REASONING
> o PRODUCTIVE PRESENTATIONS

o EFFECTIVE NEW RIGGINGS
o TECHNOLOGICAL ADVANCES

V. SHALLOW WATER BASS - Catching shallow water largemouth is not particularly difficult. Catching lots of them usually is. Even more challenging is catching lunker-size bass in seasons other than during the spring spawn. Anglers applying the information within the covers of this book on marshes, estuaries, reservoirs, lakes, creeks or small ponds should triple their results. The book details productive new tactics to apply to thin-water angling. Numerous photographs and figures easily define the optimal locations and proven methods to catch bass.

SPECIAL FEATURES
o UNDERSTANDING BASS/COVER INTERFACE
o METHODS TO LOCATE BASS CONCENTRATIONS
o ANALYSIS OF WATER TYPES
o TACTICS FOR SPECIFIC HABITATS
o LARSEN'S "FLORA FACTOR"

VI. BASS FISHING FACTS - This angler's guide to the lifestyles and behavior of the black bass is a reference source of sorts, never before compiled. The book explores the behavior of bass during pre- and post-spawn as well as during bedding season. It examines how bass utilize their senses to feed and how they respond to environmental factors. The book details how fishermen can be more productive by applying such knowledge to their bass angling. The information within the covers of this book includes those bass species, known as "other" bass, such as redeye, Suwannee, spotted, etc.

SPECIAL FEATURES
o BASS FORAGING MOTIVATORS
o DETAILED SPRING MOVEMENTS
o A LOOK AT BASS SENSES
o GENETIC INTRODUCTION/STUDIES
o MINOR BASS SPECIES & HABITATS

VII. TROPHY BASS - is focused at today's dedicated lunker hunters who find more enjoyment in wrestling with one or two monster largemouth than with a "panfull" of yearlings. To help the reader better understand how to catch big bass, a majority of this book explores productive techniques for trophies. The "how to" information was gleaned from professional guides and other experienced trophy bass hunters. This book takes a look at geographical areas and waters that offer opportunities to catch giant bass.

SPECIAL FEATURES
o GEOGRAPHIC DISTRIBUTIONS
o STATE RECORD INFORMATION

o GENETIC GIANTS
o TECHNIQUES FOR TROPHIES
o LOCATION CONSIDERATIONS
o LURE AND BAIT TIMING

VIII. AN ANGLER'S GUIDE TO BASS PATTERNS examines the most effective combination of lure, method and places. Being able to develop a pattern of successful methods and lures for specific habitats and environmental conditions is the key to catching several bass on each fishing trip. Understanding bass movements and activities and the most appropriate and effective techniques to employ will add many pounds of enjoyment to the sport of bass fishing. "Bass Patterns" is a reference source for all anglers, regardless of where they live or their skill level.

SPECIAL FEATURES
o BOAT POSITIONING
o NEW WATER STRATEGIES
o DEPTH AND COVER CONCEPTS
o MOVING WATER TACTICS
o WEATHER/ACTIVITY FACTORS
o TRANSITIONAL TECHNIQUES

IX. BASS GUIDE TIPS focuses on the productive tactics of the country's top fishing guides. Many of the guides mentioned are "trophy specialists" while others are simply "bass guides" who catch lots of largemouth. Often the guides catch trophies one day and huge numbers the next. They are all excellent anglers and professional fishermen who are dedicated to providing the best service to their clientele. The "tips" within each chapter are effective methods that will help the reader catch more and larger bass. The proven techniques discussed are applicable to most waters around the country. Many, however, are not widely known in certain parts of the country.

SPECIAL FEATURES
o SHINERS, SUNFISH KITES & FLIES
o FLIPPIN', PITCHIN' & DEAD STICKIN'
o RATTLIN', SKIPPIN' & JERK BAITS
o MOVING, DEEP, HOT & COLD WATERS
o BRACKISH WATERS & BASS SIGNS
o FRONTS, HIGH WINDS & RAIN

LARSEN'S OUTDOOR PUBLISHING
CONVENIENT ORDER FORM
ALL PRICES INCLUDE POSTAGE/HANDLING

FRESH WATER

___ BSL3.   Bass Pro Strategies   ($14.95)
___ BSL4.   Bass Lures/Tech.   ($14.95)
___ BSL5.   Shallow Water Bass ($14.95)
___ BSL6.   Bass Fishing Facts ($13.95)
___ BSL8.   Bass Patterns ($14.95)
___ BSL9.   Bass Guide Tips ($14.95)
___ CF1.   Mstrs' Scrts/Crappie Fshg ($12.95)
___ CF2.   Crappie Tactics ($12.95)
___ CF3.   Mstr's Secrets of Catfishing ($12.95)
___ LB1.   Larsen on Bass Tactics ($15.95)
___ PF1.   Peacock Bass Explosions! ($16.95)
___ PF2.   Peacock Bass & Other Fierce
                 Exotics ($17.95)
___ PF3.   Peacock Bass Addiction ($18.95)

SALT WATER

___ IL1.   The Snook Book   ($14.95)
___ IL2.   The Redfish Book ($14.95)
___ IL3.   The Tarpon Book ($14.95)
___ IL4.   The Trout Book ($14.95)
___ SW1.   The Reef Fishing Book ($16.45)
___ SW2.   Masters Bk/Snook ($16.45)

REGIONAL

___ FG1.   Secret Spots-Tampa Bay/
                 Cedar Key   ($15.95)
___ FG2.   Secret Spots - SW Florida ($15.95)
___ BW1.   Guide/North Fl. Waters ($16.95)
___ BW2.   Guide/Cntral Fl.Waters ($15.95)
___ BW3.   Guide/South Fl.Waters ($15.95)
___ OT3.   Fish/Dive Florida/Keys ($13.95)

HUNTING

___ DH1.   Mstrs' Secrets/ Deer Hunting ($14.95)
___ DH2.   Science of Deer Hunting ($14.95)
___ DH3.   Mstrs' Secrets/Bowhunting ($12.45)
___ DH4.   How to Take Monster Bucks ($13.95)
___ TH1.   Mstrs' Secrets/ Turkey Hunting ($14.95)

OTHER OUTDOORS BOOKS

___ DL2.   Manatees/Vanishing ($11.45)
___ DL3.   Sea Turtles/Watchers' ($11.45)

FREE BROCHURES

___ Peacock Bass Brochure
___ LOP Book Catalog

BIG MULTI-BOOK DISCOUNT!	INTERNATIONAL AIRMAIL ORDERS
2-3 books, SAVE 10% 4 or more books, SAVE 20%	Send check in U.S. funds; add $6 more for 1 book, $4 for each additional book

ALL PRICES INCLUDE U.S. POSTAGE/HANDLING

No. of books _____ x $_____ ea   = $_____
No. of books _____ x $_____ ea   = $_____
     Multi-book Discount   (%) $_____
SUBTOTAL $_____

☐ **Priority Mail (add $2.50 more for every 2 books)** $_____
   TOTAL   ENCLOSED   (check or money order) $_____

NAME_____ADDRESS_____

CITY_____STATE_____ZIP_____

Send check/Money Order to: Larsen's Outdoor Publishing,
Dept. BR99, 2640 Elizabeth Place, Lakeland, FL 33813
           (Sorry, no credit card orders)

LARSEN'S OUTDOOR PUBLISHING

SPECIAL OFFER: If you would like to be on our mailing list for information regarding upcoming books in the Bass Series Library, special discounts, plus information on other outdoor titles, please fill out your name below and return to:

Larsen's Outdoor Publishing
Dept. "BK9"
2640 Elizabeth Place
Lakeland, FL 33813

NAME_____

ADDRESS_____

CITY_____STATE_____ZIP_____

✄ — — — — — — — — — — — — — — — — — —

LARSEN'S OUTDOOR PUBLISHING

FOR YOUR FISHING BUDDY: If you have a friend who would be interested in receiving a free brochure with information on the Bass Series Library and other titles offered by Larsen's Outdoor Publishing, please fill out their name below and we'll send it out immediately.

FRIEND'S NAME _____

ADDRESS_____

CITY_____STATE_____ZIP_____

Larsen's Outdoor Publishing
Dept. "BK9"
2640 Elizabeth Place
Lakeland, FL 33813